All the Days
of My Life

All the Days
of My Life

by Sister Mary Jeremy

the NEW *Bobbs-Merrill* COMPANY, INC.

AN ASSOCIATE OF HOWARD W. SAMS & CO., INC.

Publishers • INDIANAPOLIS • NEW YORK

emy,

IMPRIMATUR:

✝ Martinus D. McNamara

Episcopus Joliettensis in Illinois

First Edition

TO

St. Jude

AND ALL WHO MADE POSSIBLE

All the Days of My Life.

ONE thing I have asked of the Lord,
this will I seek after;
that I may dwell in the house of the Lord
all the days of my life.

Psalms 26:4

THIS IS THE STORY OF A TEACHING SISTER.

The names of persons and
places have been changed.

All the Days
of My Life

Chapter One

You wouldn't have believed me then if I had told you. You couldn't. Besides, I don't think I would have known how to tell you. Oh, I was so much in love! After three years in the convent, I was ready and eager to pronounce my first vows as a Sister of St. Francis. Everyone thought twenty was too young to know one's mind, that it was a fleeting fancy. Yet, I sometimes think I had never known any other love. Everything had become so familiar—the friendly bell in the little steeple announcing the day's round of rising, chapel exercises, work, recreation, meals—the fourteen acres of green surrounding the solid stone buildings of my new home.

Folks had predicted this for Julianne but not for me, Clare. My attachment to Julianne, they said, drew me after her. Could it be that only three years before Julianne and I, excited and a little apprehensive, had waited in the convent parlor? How well I remembered! Julianne, her deep eyes shining, her lips parted in that eager smile of hers, looked every bit like a bride-to-be. She was always the generous heart; making sacrifices had long been a habit with her. But with me it was different. Ambitious and somewhat self-willed, I had been alternately weaving and unraveling glittering dreams of my future ever since I had first looked out a window. Yet, when the moment came—that timeless moment when God suddenly touches a soul in the place inaccessible to all but Him—when that moment came to me, I somehow arose and embraced it. Rather was it like a beautiful land stretching far into the horizon. As I imagined myself before the gateway, I suddenly knew its key was in my hand. It was the little word "Yes."

Julianne broke through my musing with: "Clare! Those chimes—aren't they beautiful?"

It was the first sound we had heard from inside the enclosure.

Later we would come to love the huge old grandfather clock with the turreted top standing beside the entrance in the main hall. Just then the large door to the enclosure opened. Mother Regina came toward us and we stood up to greet her. She was in her mid-fifties, with alert gray eyes that immediately held you, and an easy, friendly smile.

"So you are the girls from Ohio! Welcome to St. Francis. I hope you'll learn to love your new home." Her voice was kind, and she took our hands in her own. I wondered if she felt mine trembling. I was thinking of home—Dad, Mother, my brothers, who were now sitting down to supper back in Crestline, now seemingly half a planet away! For an instant I glanced across the room at the large, exquisitely carved crucifix. From far away a voice was saying, "I'm Julianne, and this is Clare, Reverend Mother." I smiled, and the gray eyes reassured me.

"Yes, and that reminds me, girls. I have the recommendation from your pastor and the transcript of your high school credits, but no other recommendation. Did you bring one from your employers, for instance?"

Julianne and I looked at each other. "Mother—" I had found my voice at last—"neither of us has ever had a job—well, not a real job, I mean. Julianne kept house for her father, and I . . ." I hesitated. Could my incorrigibly inept handling of an iron and my leaving pots to soak till later on a dance night be termed "helping?" Reverend Mother looked quizzical. I decided to use the term loosely. "I helped my mother."

Reverend Mother laughed, "Well, that takes care of that." Her chuckles made me wonder if she had indeed discerned what lay behind my hesitation.

The door opened again, and we were introduced to our Mistress, Sister Alphonse. She had very likable brown eyes and a slow but delightful smile. She led us to the chapel to make our first dedication to the God Who had chosen us. It was the wholehearted surrender of youth in its first love. Only one thing mattered: His dream for us.

Sister Alphonse then led us upstairs. In the dormitory a postulant outfit was neatly laid out for each of us. We donned the simple black dress, cape and white bonnet, laying aside our "worldly clothes," to be given back to our folks before Reception. With scarcely a backward glance at the flimsy heap of colored stuff, we found our way downstairs with the help of a friendly novice.

In her office Sister Alphonse explained our future a little further. "The first year of your religious training is called the postulancy. It is in the house of novices but separated from the formal novitiate."

"Like the lowest class private?" I ventured.

Sister Alphonse smiled. "That's right, Clare. At the end of this year if the community finds you fit and you still desire to become a religious, you will be allowed to take the veil and wear the habit of St. Francis as a novice."

"That's for two years, isn't it?" queried Julianne.

"You are correct," assented Sister. "Then the three-year period of temporary vows follows."

"You mean we're not finished yet?" I sighed.

"No, Clare. The Church, like the wise Mother she is, wants to safeguard both the candidate and the community. I'm certain you understand why a person should be as sure of her vocation as possible."

Julianne and I looked at each other. "We are sure" was in our eyes. Sister read it and continued with a smile, "Oh, you may feel sure now, but you have never tried to live as a religious, a teaching religious at that. There are all sorts of qualifications for both which you must meet."

I flipped back one side of my postulant cape; it felt new and strange. "It's beginning to sound complicated, Sister. I thought Franciscans were simple people."

"You have it there, Clare," Sister agreed. "Franciscans *are* simple. One of our great Franciscan sayings is, 'Simplicity is the daughter of truth.' And since you know humility is truth, all you have to do is to be humble, and your religious life will be the simplest thing in the world. It is always pride that complicates things."

That was the beginning of our formal instructions in religious life. They covered the whole range of spiritual perfection, from the right intention down to the tiniest detail of the vows. This, along with daily opportunities to practice what we were learning, rounded out our training.

And now we were at the end of our novitiate. After a year of probation we had received the habit of St. Francis. Julianne had become Sister Olivia and I, Sister Jeremy. Then had followed our two-year novitiate. Thus after these three years we considered ourselves old hands at anything from serving dear old Sister Thomas her daily cottage cheese to ringing the steeple bell at 5:00 a.m.

We had learned to take our meals to the tune of spiritual reading instead of to someone's joshing about who carried our books home that afternoon. We were indefatigable at the 5:30 morning meditation, and had learned a little of the spirit of recollection while working. In all its kindness, the community was accepting us today for profession.

Eternity cannot be as long as those minutes seemed that kept us from the fulfillment of our dream. The bishop was to preside. Parents, relatives and friends had traveled miles for the ceremony. The date was a traditional one, August 12. The sun's rays were intensified again by the stone on which the city of Tannerton is built. During the whole month, the cicadas incessantly screeched their forecast of the morrow's weather—hotter—and the staunch grass withered under the scorching glare of the sun. The day was typical. But only my heart showed the effects of the temperature. It swelled and pulsed until I thought that even my ample habit wouldn't contain it. As we stood in the chapel corridor, eagerly awaiting the arrival of the bishop and his retinue, listening to the organ sounding the prelude of our wedding march, I suppose the other twenty-five novices felt as I did.

Twenty-six; yes, we were twenty-six now. There had been thirty-two at first. Marie—small, sweet, docile, pining for her dear ones, every letter from home leaving her more depressed—had been advised to return home. Efficient, hard-working Margaret had left also. "Those bells," she would say. "You can't accomplish anything here—too many changes in occupation." Then there was Martha— "Why, I don't have to have people tell me when to take my next breath. This is not for me." One day in early winter her place in the postulancy had also become vacant.

"Julianne," I remember saying after one of these departures, "maybe I ought to go home, too. After all, I could do so much good in the world."

"Don't be silly, Clare," Julianne chided vigorously. "You know we always said that nothing could make us turn back. This is where God wants us to work for the salvation of our own souls and for the Christian education of youth. Just pray to Our Lady to guide and strengthen you."

"But, Julianne," I argued, "I can be a public-school teacher. Children in parochial schools already know about God. Why should we take such an interest in them?"

"Clare! How can you let the devil pull your leg like that?" Julianne, for all her gentle ways, was not above using a barb of good crisp slang to drive home her point.

And so twenty-nine of us had received the habit. In the novitiate we were trained in the vows of poverty, chastity and obedience. While attending classes in preparation for teaching, three more of the original group left.

I was disturbed again. Sister Olivia, as I had now learned to call her, rose to the occasion. "Sister Jeremy, do you want Our Lord to say to you on judgment day, 'Depart from Me—He who puts his hand to the plow and looks back is not worthy of Me'?" But death seems far away when you're twenty, and I felt that I could have done so much for Christ in the world that He would have forgotten the few years I might have spent in religious life. Gradually I saw the deception in these thoughts and put them aside for keeps.

Today was our profession day. The bishop had arrived, and as we novices led the procession down the chapel aisle, I became aware of the colorful, crowded benches. A man cleared his throat in a familiar fashion. That would be Dad. I heard someone whisper excitedly, "There's Clare," and I glimpsed a movement of white in my mother's hand. It was a year since I had seen them, and despite my three years' training, I felt an urgent impulse to break rank, run to her arms and kiss her. But the novices in front of me and Sister Olivia were moving steadily forward, and behind us the others kept an even pace. The choir was singing anticipantly, "*Veni Sponsa Christi*," and gladness thrilled through me once again. The little Gothic chapel with its capacity of four hundred could have been St. Peter's at Rome, such was our exaltation. In the sanctuary glowed the colorful robes of the bishop and monsignori; in the first pews the white, brown and black habits and cassocks of the priest guests were conspicuous. Here had assembled representatives from various ranks of the Church's clergy to acknowledge our privilege of having been chosen by Christ to do His work.

I looked at the altar, rich in white and gold cloth and lace, luxuriant with two large vases filled with deep red roses, beautiful for a King. And when I thought of my God and King, to Whom in a few minutes I would solemnly and publicly vow my love, all my homesickness vanished.

Presently we were kneeling at the altar rail, the twenty-six of us, young, happy and desperately in love. The bishop's guard of honor —his clergy and Franciscan friars—were witnesses as out of the centuries the voice of Italy's troubadour of God echoed in the words of the bishop: "My children, what is your petition?" Our voices answered without a tremor, "Right Reverend Bishop, we ask to be admitted to the vows of the Third Order Regular of St. Francis, in order to do penance, to amend our lives and to serve God faithfully until death."

For two years we had worn the religious habit, to try out in actual practice without the obligation of the vows to live the life of a Sister. But now the day of fulfillment was at hand. We were about to pledge our lives to the King's service.

"If you observe these things," the bishop concluded solemnly, "I, on the part of Almighty God, promise you life everlasting."

The better part of the bargain, I thought, had so far been on my side, rather than on God's. "These things"—to live in poverty, chastity and obedience—hadn't proved so terrible in the novitiate.

18

The time spent in training for religious life and preparation for teaching had passed like a holiday in heaven.

But today thoughts of teaching the young were far from my mind. I was in love; I had just pledged, solemnly and publicly, allegiance to God Who had claimed my heart. We had been permitted to make our first vows for a period of only one year. But I knew that in my heart I had made my vows for life. Already the phrase from the formula of perpetual vows had become my own: "All the days of my life." I was in love—nothing else mattered, nothing else counted.

The row of novices in front of us rose, and we moved forward to receive our black veils in exchange for the white ones we had worn up to now. Here at last was the beginning of the realization of our dream. The silver crucifix we would now wear set the seal on our dedication.

"Holy God, we praise Thy name." How sincerely I joined in the closing hymn!

"Where do we go from here, Sister Jeremy?" Sister Olivia asked as we came down the community stairs into the sunny yard.

"Your guess is as good as mine. It doesn't seem like three years since we made our first vows, and it can't be six since we entered. Yet, yesterday we did make perpetual profession." I looked down at the brand new ring on my finger. The plain band of gold was engraved with the Holy Name of Jesus. "I thought I'd never live to see it, another August 12. Remember my ups and downs?"

"Don't I, though? But the end is not yet. This is just the beginning. We have to pray every day to the Mother of God for perseverance in the service of her Son."

"Yes, it is a great grace. Sister Alphonse is right when she tells us to say that little prayer during elevation at Mass."

We were strolling down the maple-lined path toward the Calvary shrine. Our ubiquitous squirrels were busily burying maple seeds, and the wrens were getting in some last minute summer trills. I looked over the broad green expanse. For six happy years this had been home. I turned to Sister Olivia, and her eyes met mine. Our friendship had been strengthened by a deeper spiritual insight as we grew together in the love of God. "It was grand of Mother Regina to keep us both home till we had our degree. Do you think, my fair English major, that you and this little science major might go to the same mission?"

She laughed. "Quit pinning your hopes so high. Tonight will tell. Mother Regina's notice said that at eight o'clock she will give us our appointments for the coming year. After that we are to retire in silence and pray for the spirit of true obedience."

"Just like you—you've got it all by heart!" I laughed. We stood a moment at the crucifix under the vine-covered roof. "I wish tonight were here. I want to know where I'm going."

"Why do you always wish your life away? Let's enjoy these last remaining hours."

"Just think!" I continued, not heeding her admonition. "There are about a hundred things we could be assigned to do."

"Hmm, you sure think you're efficient, Sister Jeremy. Give me air."

"All right, there are fifty missions. English majors can't add, so let me explain. At each one of these missions there ought to be at least two teaching jobs we could fill. That makes one hundred possibilities."

"I'll show you I remember the math course I took, even if it was required. Besides teaching, we could be cook or sacristan at each place. That makes a total of two hundred jobs, plus the possibility of being a janitor. Of course, you would not contemplate being principal?" She flashed a mischievous eye, but before I could answer, the bell rang for chapel.

That day the hours seemed like years for us, the uninitiated. The seasoned teachers were wondering whether Sister Theresa would be returning to teach, or be appointed companion to Sister Felicia attending Catholic University. Others wondered whether Sister Basil would fill the vacancy left by the retiring principal Sister Louise. And so speculations ran rampant. To me all this was befuddling; I didn't know one fifth of the seven hundred members of the community, much less the places of their previous assignments. I had never thought that appointment night could arouse so much excitement. My pulse fluttered like a vigil light.

As Sister Olivia and I took our seats in the front row of the auditorium together with the other fledglings, I was greeted with a series of lopsided smiles. We were there first. We were not going to miss anything. The silence was profound. Only the rustle of habits and the occasional slight jingle of rosary beads announced the entrance of the older Sisters. It was a quiet, muffled group.

Like an army at attention, the entire body arose in salutation to the Superior General, as Mother Regina, with firm, even gait, came down the main aisle and ascended the steps to the stage. To remind us that we had pledged to accept cheerfully our appointments in His name and for His cause, a large crucifix had been placed on the stage. The invocation by Mother Regina for God's blessing on our efforts, and for strength in accomplishing our duty, was answered fervently. After a few words of admonition, Mother Regina, in a clear and unmistakably decisive tone began reading the appointments. The list was arranged alphabetically by diocese and parish. After an interminable recitation of names, I heard "Sister Jeremy" and found myself on the faculty of St. Albert's High School in an Ohio city. I heard no more. Sister Olivia, Sister Olivia, I tried to recall—when did Mother Regina call her name? How selfish of me just to listen for my own name! Sister Olivia handed me a slip of paper: "St. Francis, Chicago."

I had no recollection of leaving the auditorium, but I do remember that I spent the night imagining a variety of classrooms, schools, principals and superintendents, until I dozed into a fitful sleep filled with undisciplined classes, havoc, unprepared lectures and irate parents. The early rising bell was very welcome. The morning meditation, Office of the Blessed Virgin Mary and Holy Mass seemed very long in my eagerness to be about my Father's business. We had a hurried breakfast, and by eight-fifteen were ready to start for the station.

The taxis were lined up in the convent courtyard. About fifty of us were leaving on the early train.

"Sister Jeremy, it looks as if you are the only brand-new Sister going out on mission today." Mother Regina was smiling at me. "Is this your luggage?" Mother said it partly to me but mostly to the accumulation of impedimenta—packages, parcels, sacks, bags and baggage at my feet and in my arms.

"Yes, Mother," I stammered.

"Don't you have a trunk, dear?"

I was wishing Mother would talk to the others who were gradually assembling in groups in the court. "Oh, yes, Mother."

"Where is it?"

"Oh, it went off this morning, Sister Superior said," I chattered. "It was less weight than needed to go on my ticket."

"But why didn't you put these things into it, dear?"

"Well, I need some of these things right away and maybe my trunk won't come for a long time. Then Sister Amelia asked me to take this to her little nephew and Sister Adrian wanted to know if I would mind carrying just this little bag [ten-pound sack] for her sister, Sister Marie, who is at the mission I'm going to. I promised to do about ten of these little errands."

She seemed disturbed as she asked, "Sister, is your suitcase filled?"

Reverend Mother answered my muteness by taking my suitcase and opening it. There the toothbrush was hurtling over coif and missal in an attempt to stay put in the loosely packed case. With a little maneuvering, she fitted several of the parcels inside.

"There now, that's better, isn't it, Sister Jeremy?" Mother Regina said triumphantly. "Next time you don't have to play American Express Company to the community. There is such a thing as extremes in everything. Well, here is our future Chicagoan, Sister Olivia, to say good-by."

Mother's kindness made the lump that I had been pushing down for hours rise again. I merely grunted a scarcely audible "Thank you," afraid to look at Sister Olivia. The lump had already aspirated a few wet blobs around my eyes. I hid my face in her veil as she kissed me. There was no need to speak. Sister Olivia squeezed my hand and then turned and left the court.

"Now, Sister Ida, here is Sister Jeremy." Mother had come back with a tall, broad Sister whom till then I had known only by sight. "Sister Jeremy is just the Sister you will want to entrust with the taxi fare." I had long since learned to expect a sly little joke from Mother Regina.

"Thank you, Mother, and good-by," we said as Mother Regina went back into the building with Sister Olivia.

"Sister Jeremy," Sister Ida instructed, "there are three taxis for the eleven of us for St. Albert's. Here's a purse."

I had not held a purse for six years, but I supposed they worked the same as always. I grasped the black zippered bag gingerly and clung to it as if I might have it snatched away by one of these fifty Franciscan Sisters who had just made or renewed their vows, including poverty.

I noticed the placards on the taxis stating they were five-cent taxis. Times must have changed since I left the world six years ago. A tremendous deflation must have taken place, although I could not remember having heard about it in the current events class of the summer session. Or perhaps this was a special taxi for religious orders who had vowed poverty. When we reached the station, everyone bustled out of the taxis carrying some of my luggage. With aplomb I counted out fifteen cents—five cents for each taxi. The drivers' faces showed utter amazement and consternation, which I interpreted as surprise that I had paid them at all.

At recreation that night I was to hear the incident recounted with high hilarity and an appalling lack of sympathy for my apparent "other-worldliness." Oh, well, *somebody* has to provide occasions for taxi drivers to prove themselves noble gentlemen.

Finally we were on the eastbound train out of Chicago, but no streamliner could have kept pace with my anticipations. Taking advantage of the uneven number of Sisters, I sat alone, struggling with the pangs of separation from Sister Olivia. My eyes burned as I blinked at the passing scenery.

I recalled how Sister Olivia, unknown to me, had prepared me for this day. We had been together twenty-four years in all. This was like leaving home again. It was not only a separation from a life-long friend, but from the convent home we had both come to

23

love. In the past six years from postulancy days, through the novitiate and our three years as Sisters of temporary vows, Sister Olivia had been vigilant. When I fretted because we had not been appointed to the same work, Sister Olivia would say, "Sister Jeremy, we came to be religious, to be obedient, not to enjoy each other's company. Go do your work with the others even if you don't like it. What makes you think you are angelic to work with?" I would leave rather reluctantly. If we were placed together or with a group, Sister Olivia was always on guard not to show me any preference, so that I often wondered if she remembered we had been schoolmates. Now I began to see how wise she had been to prepare me for the inevitable separation.

I felt like an aviator on his initial solo flight. Although I thought I was qualified for any teaching position to which I would be assigned, I had never been on any mission. I had a Bachelor of Science degree and all the educational hours required for a high school teacher in the state of Ohio. The qualifications were complete, even to the point of the religious life. Twenty-four hours ago, I had made my final vows: "I, Sister Mary Jeremy, vow to Almighty God, to live all the days of my life . . ." Yes, all the days of my life. The ring on my left hand served as a constant reminder of my unending dedication to Christ. I had a ring and a degree. Both were to prove indispensable, particularly during those first years of teaching.

"Do you mind if I sit next to you, Sister Jeremy?" a very pleasant young voice said.

"Thanks be to God," I said under my breath, "I have myself under control." Yet I hardly trusted myself to look from the window. I nodded a welcome to Sister Martin and tried to move from the other half of the seat the parcels and boxes in my care. Sister Martin, I had learned, was second grade teacher at St. Albert's and a kind of volunteer public relations manager.

"What do you think you'll teach at Saint Albert's, Sister?" Sister Martin's eyes flashed as she took her place next to me. She looked kind, but my nostalgic mood had the better of me.

"I don't know."

"Well, you have a degree. Aren't you ready for anything?"

"I suppose I'll teach chemistry and physics. Science is my major. I am not prepared for anything else—well, not so well prepared. I love science."

"I'll tell you—" Sister Martin came closer, speaking confidentially—"you don't always get what you expect. Sister Basil, the principal, might try you out. Both Sister Ida and Father Murphy teach the sciences and they are both back. Maybe you'll teach the grades. And I tell you, don't argue about it. Sister Basil is like this: if she calls you *Sister*, then the calm is on. If she calls you *Sister Jeremy*, it is still safe. But I tell you, if it is *Sister Mary Jeremy*, then you'd better examine your conscience."

"I'm not afraid," I replied disinterestedly, and kept looking more out of the window than in the direction of my companion.

"St. Albert's is a parochial grade and high school," Sister Martin chattered on, "the oldest in the diocese. You know Lincoln helped make the bricks, Abe himself." I turned quickly and I looked at her incredulously. "Well, *maybe* he did," she corrected. "Father Becker, the pastor, is the superintendent of the school and also the dean of the diocese. He's so busy that Sister Basil has full authority in the school. St. Albert's High has an 'A' rating from the Ohio State Department of Education. Some quite impressive civic leaders and businessmen and women have had their beginning there. What's the matter with you, Sister Jeremy? Don't you ever say any more than this? You're not one of those quiet ones, are you?"

"Oh, no, I'm happy to hear about where I'm going," I encouraged shakily.

"Oh, you'll learn to like it. You're from Ohio, aren't you?"

"Yes, of course, but I have been away long enough to be weaned."

"Let's see, where was I? Oh, yes, it's also a very poor place. Lady Poverty reigns, and our Holy Father St. Francis would find it quite to his taste, I think. The streets around St. Albert's neighborhood are narrow, and the side walks merely brick-laid paths."

All this did not make any impression on my homesick mood.

We arrived at sunset. After a brief ride the taxi stopped before a nondescript house on a street of nondescript houses. Beside it towered an ancient stone building which obviously antedated even

25

the old train station we had just left. I thought perhaps they were stopping over for lunch, so I followed the others.

A kindly-looking Sister, whom they greeted as Sister Marie, opened the door of the house and with a graceful movement ushered the eleven of us into the community room saying in a jolly voice, "Welcome back to St. Albert's" and "Welcome, Sister Jeremy," as I struggled with the parcels, one of which I recalled was for her.

All parochial schools have living accommodations for their religious teachers. Accommodations? Well—yes, if one does not include in the term all the desired or convenient facilities for living. The word accommodation I found was quite an elastic term.

The community room was about twenty-five by twelve feet, and contained three long homemade tables arranged lengthwise. There were twenty-eight faculty members; floor space and budget vetoed individual desks. Each table was fitted with a series of drawers, one for each Sister, to hold her immediate necessities. Each faculty member occupied a specified place at the table. The principal sat at the head of the first table with faculty members to the right and to the left, according to seniority all the way down to the twenty-eighth at the end of the table. I was given the seat at the foot of the table facing the principal. It really was an enviable position. One more mature might not have thought so, and would have developed enough self-consciousness to find this box seat undesirable. But I noticed that all those occupying the sides of the table often had to crane their necks to see the principal or a Sister a few places removed, while I, at the foot of the table, did not miss a thing. I could look straight at the principal and could see the faculty to her right or her left. I could watch everyone's expression as various discussions went on, serious or gay. Also, I could enjoy the view through the three windows. It was very pleasant to be the youngest faculty member.

The community room had many uses. We assembled here for recreation. Here the senior members initiated us in the art of teaching and of living on a mission. During periods of relaxation, we mended our clothing, did needlework, prepared posters for class-

26

room use, with hardly elbow space for any of us. It was remarkable what pieces of art we developed in the course of time.

The room was also our study. In it we prepared our lessons, corrected papers, typed examinations and cut stencils for course outlines and programs. Here, too, we held our faculty meetings. The room was a melting pot of activities and saw us display chameleonlike qualities, from the strictly formal behavior at faculty meetings to the irrepressible gaiety of evening and holiday recreations.

"Today is the day, Sister Jeremy," Sister Martin informed me after breakfast on August 16, as she was reading the notice Sister Basil had just posted in the community room. "Let me know right after the meeting what it is going to be."

"You seem more anxious than I, Sister," I said, trying to cover my nervousness.

The high school faculty assembled in the Sisters' community room to receive class and course appointments for the scholastic year. My moment had come. Now I would learn what subjects would be assigned to me. My hopes soared.

There was no warning note in the principal's voice as she read the appointments to the high school faculty that fateful August day. I felt certain that my appointment would be mathematics, chemistry and physics. Mentally I was arranging the laboratories for my classes and paid little attention to the words of the principal. The steady drone of her voice suddenly touched my auditory nerves: "Junior Class, Physics, Sister Mary Ida." My shock subsided with the realization that Sister Mary Ida was an outstanding science teacher and also a Bachelor of Science with a minor in physics. Agitation made me alert. Now the senior classes were being assigned. Here it comes, I thought. "Senior Class, Chemistry, Sister Mary Ida."

This was preposterous. My name had not even been mentioned on the faculty list. I remembered Sister Martin's warning.

What if I did not belong here? What if this were not my first mission? I felt that I must see the principal immediately after the meeting.

The principal, Sister Basil, was a woman of more than average stature and of military bearing. What she said she meant; there was no retracting. One acted. It was but an interval, for example, between a state inspector's meeting her and the school's receiving an "A" rating. The principal had already been in the classroom as a novice of sixteen, and was a principal in her early twenties. Now at sixty she was still the principal. Her years of experience had enriched her understanding of problems involved in school administration.

Every look she had given me since my arrival at the mission had revealed her lack of confidence in my disciplinary ability. That was to be expected, but I certainly had not figured on being counted out all together. My father was a small man, and I was my father's daughter, but my father was also a fearless man and I was my father's daughter.

As soon as some of the senior faculty members had completed their transactions, I ventured into the principal's office. She was seated at her desk, and even there she was towering. I felt like a little girl at a candy counter selecting a penny's worth of mixed hard tack. With uncanny foresight, she addressed me.

"Sister Mary Jeremy," she said, "I thought it better if you take the freshman classes in Latin and German. I am afraid that you would find the laboratory courses too difficult to discipline during your first year. Father Murphy will continue helping Sister Ida."

In my presumption I had not even heard the names of the freshman instructors. The only thing I could remember was an assignment I had once been given in a college rhetoric class to describe the feeling of a person diving off a two-hundred-foot embankment. Never having performed such a feat I had found the task somewhat difficult. Now I could have made an "A plus" on the theme. This was the most convincing experience of precipitation I had ever had.

I wanted to tell the principal that my major was science, my minor mathematics, that—but I remembered that the authorities at dear old Alma Mater had seen to it that, since I was to teach high school, I should get sixteen hours in as many subjects as possible.

28

German and Latin had been among them. Happily, of a sudden I realized the true symbolism of my ring. It involved among other things absolute obedience to my lawful superiors.

"That will be all, Sister Mary Jeremy," Sister Basil said with finality.

I stumbled out of the office, almost falling into Sister Martin's arms.

"I know. I saw the schedule. But you'll like it," she soothed, as we stood at the window of the community room overlooking the schoolyard.

How I was wishing for Sister Olivia! She would know just what to do or how to act. But I knew we would not write until Christmas, for our Rule does not approve of much correspondence.

"Look out there, Sister Jeremy." Sister Martin pointed down into the schoolyard. Within the range of my vision came two bobbing heads, one with a shock of blond curls, the other with straight, disheveled, startling red hair. My eyes moved slowly down the lively, grinning faces, past the open-throated shirts to the overalls rolled just below the knee and the size ten bare feet. "All the days of my life" echoed somewhere in my subconscious. What would I do for even one day with such fellows?

Sister Martin soon enlightened me. "That's Red and Pete."

I knew one Pete around St. Albert's, our cigar-smoking, besmudged janitor, Pete Powilski.

"Pete is the janitor's son," Sister Martin went on, "and Red's dad is a policeman."

"You mean those two antiquarians," I stammered, "are still in high school?"

"Easy, easy, Sister," soothed Sister Martin. "They have sophomore standing in everything except German and Latin." Then she winked and pinched my chin. "Sufficient for the day is the anticipation thereof."

Only when I saw Red and Pete the first day in class did I recover from shock. They were reconditioned, spotless in white shoes and white suit, hair slicked down smoothly. They were the two sophomores reassigned to Freshman Latin and German.

My large class of forty-five fitted snugly in the bungalow room. I might also say smugly, for I was a young Sister and many were planning my downfall. The low windows opened into the courtyard through which five hundred grade children passed to and from school. Out of these windows my students managed to distribute forgotten hankies and other sundries to their little brothers and sisters or to the neighbors' children. The rear left corner of the room housed the old potbellied stove which, as I was to learn, had never been thermostatically controlled. Only by changing position and distance from the stove could one attain some semblance of comfort. Along the back wall ranged hangers for wraps. The hangers were rather useless, since the wraps more often were draped around the backs of the students in the last benches. Four double rows of desks ran close up to the instructor's desk and flat against the other wall. My vantage point was behind my desk. Only the front blackboard was available. On this I had written a column of German words.

I took it in a lordly manner that first day of school. I was Caesar, Napoleon, Alexander the Great, master of all I surveyed. But soon I realized that something more than surveying had to be done. There were already signs of a slight uprising in the ranks. I tried to recall the proper procedure for such occasions from method class lectures, but to no avail. I had recourse to the few things I could remember from my own high school days. I had admired the instructors who could associate my name with my face after the first meeting. The principal had given us the list for our various classes. Since the German class was the first I was to meet, I had attempted to memorize the roster: Eberberger, Efflein, Fleishman, Hirtz, Holtzapfel and MacNamara. What a task! The list continued to Weisgerber, Veerhoff.

I called student after student to repeat the list of German words, but the unrest became more pronounced. By a sleight-of-foot trick, the girl immediately behind Red was sitting on her legs, her eyes fixed in horror on the floor near the desk ahead. I followed her gaze. So that was it! Thank the Lord my brothers had long ago trained me in "mousology." Into my pencil box, schoolbag and pockets they had not seldom put one of these squirming creatures. Yes, Red had a mouse, a mouse controlled by a string tied to its hind leg. He was letting the animal creep to the teacher's desk and then pulling it back to his place. Extra adrenals would have been welcome, but pedagogy advised no feuding the first day, only gentle control. The fascinated class gloated over my ill-concealed discomfort. But suddenly I was my father's daughter again (and my brothers' sister). I coldly refused to take notice of the intruder and continued to emphasize the correct German pronunciation. Tremors in the volume, however, soon advised immediate action. I put on a sweet smile and looked down at the helpless mouse. "My dear *Mus musculus,* this is the German class—you must be lost. I'm sure your kind guardian will be happy to take you over to the biology class." Then, while a faint snickering ventured on the tensioned air, I caught Red in the eye with *"Raus mit der mus! Mach schnell!"*

A dumbfounded Red stumbled from the room with *Mus musculus,* as the snickers broke into hearty laughter. "All the days of my life . . ." Here then, the "days" were to start.

I taught Latin and German, but dreamed of teaching science. I drilled case endings until they stood up in my alphabet soup. I was successful: the students knew their personal endings. My success in other phases of language teaching, however, was not so marked. I showed the principal a typical examination paper in which the student had been required to write the synopsis of a Latin word. Peter was "slow"; he balanced his lack of intelligence with avoirdupois. But Peter knew his endings all right. He had written *"synopsbo, synopsbis, synopsbit."* Sister Basil said it was just Peter, Jr., and sent me back to teach more language.

Conjugations, I thought—that's what I must dwell on. I must concentrate on conjugations.

We concentrated. And in the next examination which I duly presented to Sister Basil, Freddie, who had a higher I.Q. than Peter, Jr., had joined his German auxiliary with the Latin stem. Sister Basil read aloud painfully: *"Ich will amare; du willst amare, wir wollen amare, sie wollen amare."*

More than ever I hoped for science. In my spiritual life obedience was sticking out like a sore thumb.

"Sister Mary Jeremy," the principal said one day, three months later (even reproof for failure was endurable in the hope of a laboratory course), "Sister Jeremy, your students are well trained in the technicalities of the language. Now you must teach them an appreciation, so that they learn to distinguish between them."

That day the ring seemed heavy on my finger. I was still my father's daughter, but neither I nor my father was a linguist. Fortunately not all my pupils were like Peter and Freddie. Many of them, immigrants or children of immigrants, spoke German fluently, more so than I, who had only an average reading knowledge of it. Peter and Freddie and all the others went to work learning an appreciation of Latin and German, or at least the difference between the two languages.

It was the last week before Christmas vacation; the principal and I were walking in the school court. Shuffling toward us came one of my linguists. Now I could demonstrate the rapid strides we had made. Hopefully I greeted my student with "*Wie gehts*, Red?"

Red looked at me abashed. "Sister, you forgot I don't take Latin no more."

That did it. The next day Sister Basil called me to her office. "Next semester, Sister Mary Jeremy," she ordered, "you will teach science."

With jubilation I included in my lesson plan for the next day "*Grosser Gott wir Loben Dich*" and none sang it more ardently than I.

Chapter Two

Brrrrrr, Brrrrrr, Brrrr.

"Mailman!" cried Sister Martin as she dashed out of the community room. Sister Basil, sitting at her place at the head of the community table checking report cards, turned to look at the disappearing Sister Martin.

In no time Sister Martin was back with both arms full of first, second, third and fourth class mail. "Looks like a rainfall, Sister Basil," she puffed.

"I thought it was a cyclone," revised Sister Basil, tongue in cheek.

Sister Martin caught the implication. "Oh, I'm sorry, Sister. I guess I do rush around too much."

Sister Marie was machine-hemming dish towels at a tremendous speed. I was at my place opposite Sister Basil, doodling while waiting for Sister Ida. I was hoping there'd be a letter from Sister Olivia. We had agreed that I would write at Christmas, so it was about time for her letter. It was the first Saturday in January and a big day in my life. My career as a science teacher was about to begin. Today Father Murphy and Sister Ida would initiate me into my new duties. Both welcomed the idea of an assistant, which was lucky for me. What seemed still luckier was that they both had attained a high degree of efficiency. Being young and aquiver with ambition, I had the temerity to presume that in a few weeks I could acquire a like skill.

As Sister Basil sorted the first class mail, we sat expectantly. The only sound was that of Sister Marie's sewing machine.

From the corner of my eye, I saw Sister Basil look up.

"Sister Mary Martin, would you be reading the diocesan paper? How did you get it already? I just put it into the rack. In all respects for your elders, you could have waited to see if anyone else wanted to read it first."

"Yes, Sister Basil," murmured the culprit with wide-eyed contrition. And she turned to Sister Marie: "Would you like to read *The Register?*"

Sister Marie waved her aside without slowing down the machine. Sister Martin gave me one of her foolish, syrupy smiles, obviously pleased to note that I, at least, was her junior. She settled herself more comfortably on the straight back chair and continued reading ... for one minute.

"Pardon me, Sister Basil, but look! It says here that Father Murphy is being transferred to St. Benedict's." She hurried over and laid the paper before the principal.

"Well, Sister Jeremy"—and I was astonished to note Sister Basil's obvious amusement—"this *is* news! Here's where you come in for the lion's share." She handed the paper back to Sister Martin, while I tried to recover from the shock.

"But really, Sister Martin," remarked the principal in an afterthought, "for a young religious, for *any religious*," she corrected, "you manage to know too much gossip. It indicates a lack of recollection."

"Yes, Sister Basil." Sister Martin sighed and turned to the obituary column.

Just then Sister Bonaventure appeared in the doorway saying, "Sister Basil, your phone is ringing."

"Thank you, Sister. I'll get it." Sister Basil rose but turned at the door with a half-smile. "Maybe it's the good padre extending his sympathy in our bereavement."

Sister Martin pulled her nose out of the paper. "Mmm, I smell something powerful good from the kitchen. Sister Bonaventure, you dear, devil's food cake?"

Sister Bonaventure was the senior housekeeper. She was nearing seventy, but nothing could stop her from working. Her beautiful face wrinkled in a grateful smile. "You little flatterer. It smells about done. I'd better see to it." She turned. "Oh, pardon me, Sister Ida, I didn't notice you there in the doorway."

"Quite all right, Sister," replied Sister Ida. "I just wanted to tell

Sister Jeremy I'm ready. Sister Jeremy, I'm sorry to have kept you waiting."

By now Sister Martin's effervescent disposition had bounced back from the recent rebuke. She bounded up to Sister Ida and thrust the paper into her hands. "Read this—Extra! Extra!"

Sister Ida had scarcely opened her mouth in surprise as she read when Sister Basil called, "Sister Ida, will you please step into the office? Sister Jeremy too."

I snatched a glance at Sister Martin and received an "I told-you-so-watch-if-I'm-not-right" look.

February had seemed so far away. I had been haunted by a million and one reasons why I might lose my coveted post as science teacher. But now time became streamlined. All Father Murphy's laboratory duties would fall to me. Not only would I be a full-time science instructor, but procurator of the lab as well. I had hoped for science, but this generous portion was beyond my expectations.

"Don't you live here any more?" asked Sister Martin as I entered the community room one afternoon in late February.

"Sister Martin, you know that the laboratory is my meat and drink and sleep. I have to acquaint myself with equipment, check condition of apparatus, take inventory, prepare lists of requirements and study and plan my lessons."

The laboratory, situated in the brick building sandwiched between the senior and freshmen bungalows, was approximately twenty-two by thirty-six feet. It was well planned for compactness and service, and adaptable to all the science classes. Two twelve-foot chemistry tables ran parallel along the north half of the room. On the south side, perpendicular to the chemistry tables, were three ten-foot physics tables. Between the chemistry and the physics divisions and opposite the instructor's desk, stood a five-foot square service table.

We had to accommodate a maximum number of students, which is putting it mildly. But I had planned my maneuvers according to standard teaching methods under Sister Ida's guidance.

35

The first day of the second semester was my red letter day. It initiated me into the field of science teachers and science students. On that February 1 (I'll never forget it) a small regiment invaded the laboratory and gathered around the physics tables. As I entered, they arose in a body. Imagine my surprise when the company saluted me lustily, "*Guten Morgen, Schwester.*" For the roster of General Science students included Fred, Red, Pete, all sophomores.

I detailed "Emily Post" rules for the laboratory, and paired partners, casually mentioning in my inexperience the method of checking each locker article against their laboratory list. In a few moments I regretted my imprudence.

As the students walked to the tables, my heart thumped with pride at my disciplinary success, even if to them each piece of equipment was only a new toy, strange but intriguing. The parade spiraled the tables as it moved toward the instructor's desk. There was no beginning or end to it. Each student brought up each piece of apparatus from his locker and held it up asking, "What is this, Sister Jeremy?" In desperation I called for attention, told them to diagram each article and use their books to identify it. I would spend days trying to decipher the results, but for the present I had devised a way to prevent the teacher from being stampeded.

The new plan was made and put into operation at once. When the next division appeared, I acquainted the students with every piece of apparatus before giving them locker privileges. I demonstrated my lesson with actual equipment and corresponding charts.

"This is a crucible," I said, showing the class a specimen of the little porcelain cup. Then I pointed to the chart to impress them with the spelling of "porcelain." "And this," I continued, "is a four-inch evaporating dish." Just then Sister Ida stepped in. Subconsciously I was aware that I had omitted something. But what? Oh, I know! I had not shown my students the lid for the crucible. Still holding the four-inch dish, I cautiously picked up a one-inch lid, saying, "and this is the crucible lid," and proceeded to fit it on the vessel. It fell to the bottom with an unholy clink.

"Isn't a lid supposed to stay on top?" softly asked a freckled-faced girl whom I was to know as Eugenia.

In mute embarrassment I nodded and quickly changed the subject.

Military tactics may be all right on battlefields, but are not always the best classroom techniques. Appointing laboratory partners, for instance, may turn out to be less wise than letting a student work with someone of his own choice. There was Fred, the quarterback, whom I had matched with Eugenia, a quiet, scholarly, meticulous girl. Fred was all muscle and supressed energy, from his bristly hair down to his springy step. Bespectacled Eugenia was mousy and not much to look at. Her slow but exact ways annoyed Fred in the day-after-day grind. The crisis came one afternoon when we were preparing oxygen. Eugenia had Fred collect apparatus, while she laboriously and painstakingly assembled it. When he tried to help, she brushed him aside. Fred stood on one foot and then the other, toying with a piece of glass tubing. Eugenia took it from him.

"What's the matter with you dames?" he asked. "Can't a guy even hold a piece of glass?"

"I need it," she said curtly.

"You girls," he grunted, "are always needin' stuff."

"Well," she asserted, "we need a right-angle bend."

"Lemme bend it," he pleaded, but Eugenia, without replying, heated and bent it herself.

"Why doncha learn your geometry?" he mumbled. "That's an obtuse angle."

Eugenia ignored him and set the bend aside to cool, oblivious to the fact that Fred was getting hotter and hotter. Wetting the glass bend, his partner worked it delicately into the one-hole stopper and set up the rest of the apparatus. She went to the dispensing table to weigh, with deliberate care, three and one half grams of potassium chlorate and one and one half grams of manganese dioxide. In the interim Fred critically eyed the setup. The burner had not yet been attached; he decided to be useful. But temptation overwhelmed him. The gas and water jets were adjacent. All his long suffering demanded recompense, and here was an opportunity. He took the burner hose and fastened it to the water supply. Red,

37

next to him, caught the action and started a grapevine message. Eugenia returned, placed the chemicals in the generator, lighted a match, carefully turned the key. A fountain of water spurted into her face. Forty members of the class roared boisterously. Eugenia, dripping and shaking in consternation, wondered whether she had struck liquid gas.

The preparation of oxygen usually furnished exciting experiences. On one occasion everything seemed under control when a swishing sound, followed by a series of slight explosions accompanied by an odor of sulphur, turned all eyes to the blob on the ceiling and then to the source. There in the farther corner stood two apparently unimpeachable students, distressed at the results of their endeavors.

"What did you put into that generator?" I asked, after I had plowed through the group surrounding them.

"Just what it says," answered Pete shakily.

"Are you sure?" I questioned.

"Yes, Sister Jeremy, we followed all the directions."

"Some impurities may have been in the generator," I said. "When you clean this and the generator, you may start over."

Fifteen minutes later we had a repetition of the fracas. This I did not take so mildly. Going back, I said in no sweet tones: "Do you really think this is funny?"

"N-n-n-o, Sister Jeremy, but honest to gosh, we put into it just what the experiment called for."

"That being what?" I demanded.

"Look, Sister," he said, as he pointed to the top of the experiment sheet. My eyes glazed as I read down the list of materials needed for each separate step of the experiment: 3.5 g. $KClO_3$, 1.5 g. MnO_2, pinch of sulphur, iron filings, a lump of charcoal.

"You couldn't!" I wilted.

"You said," he persisted, "we should always get all our materials for the whole experiment right away, and we did."

They had dumped the equivalent of a Fourth of July torpedo into their generator. Had a magnesium ribbon been listed we would all have gone through the roof. As we cleaned up the debris, I kept remembering that I had hoped for science "All the days of my life."

These cares did not disturb my youthful slumbers as much as one might expect. I knew that the One Whose ring I wore would care for me as for the "falling sparrow." But occasionally, I did become discouraged.

"Sister Ida," I confessed one evening in mid-March, after a very trying day in the laboratory, "I don't think I'll work out at all as a science teacher. Should I ask Sister Basil for another job?"

Sister Ida stared at me in amazement. She knew I loved science. "Sister Jeremy, keep your wits. Sister Basil would certainly tell you. You don't have to inform her of your incompetence. Don't be discouraged. Life is made of skirmishes; every one, if properly fought, ought to bring us closer to God."

"Yes, I know, Sister Ida, but do I take them the right way? I get so impatient. Surely this must shock my students sometimes. Then maybe they make mistakes because I haven't explained clearly enough."

Sister Ida leaned over and patted my hand. "Sister Jeremy, we're all human. Do your best and pray for light. Ask the students if everything is clear to them. If they don't state their difficulty, you can do no more. Have them discuss their problems in class. This encourages others to ask questions. However, be aware of other troubles they might have because of their personalities or environment. An after-school talk can be very helpful both character-wise and scholastically."

The longer I was procurator of the laboratory, the more I realized the lab was also a faculty supply and utility room. Here the journalism staff kept its cuts, the athletic association its uniforms, the Sodality its supplies, and the library its surplus books. In the spring our clientele increased. Each morning, students invaded the laboratory, emptying yesterday's altar flowers into our crocks and filling vases with fresh water at the sinks.

We were cramped for space, but as true Franciscans made the best of it with light hearts. Things were not as bad as at Rivo Torto long ago when St. Francis had chalked each brother's name on the rafters of the tiny hut. I had much to learn from my Sisters, veterans as they were in living the poverty we had vowed.

Pete, the janitor, was also our patron. A small, wiry man of about sixty was Pete. He walked stooped, head first, his deep-set gray-blue eyes peering through you.

"Pete," Sister Basil reprimanded, as they both walked into the laboratory one Saturday morning, "these typewriters are to be transferred to the typing room immediately. They are too heavy for Sister Jeremy, and I told you yesterday morning that they were delivered in here by mistake."

"Me, Pete, Sister Baseel?" he gesticulated, poking himself audibly in the chest. "I, janitor, no mover. I keep keys, I lock, I open."

"Pete, we will not go into that. The typewriters are to be moved immediately," Sister Basil affirmed. With that Pete knelt in front of Sister Basil, reached out his bony hand to grasp hers and attempted to kiss it. He persisted in following this European custom, a gesture of respect for religious. Sister Basil moved away, lifted a typewriter and proceeded to the typing room with it.

"I'll help you, Sister," I said.

Pete was plodding out of the laboratory, but he turned, grabbed a typewriter and kept up the refrain as he moved the machines one by one to the typing room: "I, janitor, I keep keys, I lock school, I lock church, I open school, I open church, I no move typewriters." Sister Basil had left a long time before, and the refrain was wasted on my ears.

For Pete, "janitor" meant "Keeper of the Keys," and that he was. At an hour which varied daily he would open or close all doors on the premises, unaware that we might want to enter the building earlier or work overtime. Moreover, every morning at six, from the first of November to the first of April, and regardless of weather, he would kindle a feeble fire in the potbellied stoves in the six temporary bungalow rooms. And freeze we would when classes opened if we had not added a few lumps of coal at seven in the morning before our breakfast.

Pete had learned one thing in America—the units of length. One day in demonstrating the relationship between the metric and English system of linear measurements, I explained to the class: "You see, students, the meter is about three inches longer than the yard," and proceeded to place a yardstick over the meter stick. To my dismay, they were the same length. There was a muffled snickering. Just then Pete passed the open door. Seeing the sticks in my hand, he grinned, "Seester, that new yard measure, no goot. Pete cut. You glad, Seester?"

I bowed acknowledgment. Approve I could not, and reproof would have been useless. If I was not happy, Pete was.

As semester followed semester, I appreciated Sister Ida's advice that practical demonstrations made theory easier to teach. Students retained it better. This was my third year as chemistry teacher, and my optimism was high. Having lectured to the senior class in chemistry on the value of carbon dioxide as a fire extinguisher, I decided one day to let the students kindle a fire in the metal waste basket and then put it out. As an added feature they might recharge the extinguisher, thus acquiring information on the source of the carbon dioxide. "Now, Red," I said, "you may be main demonstrator and recharger tomorrow. Select your assistant." Red chose Pete, Jr. "Both of you," I remarked, "have your preparation checked by me at the latest tomorrow morning before classes."

When it was time for the demonstration, the class assembled at a safe range around the basket while Red kindled the fire. Pete, Jr., eager to demonstrate his ability as fire chief, held the extinguisher. He was doing splendidly, when the door to the court swung open and Pete, Sr., ran in shouting, "Fire! Fire! Save boy." In a twinkling Papa had filled his coal bucket with water and dumped it on the blazing basket. I could not help wishing Pete, Sr., had been so handy a week before, when there had been an unplanned fire and he was nowhere to be found.

Another frequent occurrence which severely taxed my patience involved Mr. Simmons, the athletic director. "Just a minute, Sister Jeremy," Mr. Simmons would say entering the laboratory by the court door, waving a three-by-five card at me. "Sister Basil said I might make an announcement. You don't mind?"

41

What could I do? Repeatedly I had told him that the lab was not a good place psychologically for announcements. The students never knew what he was saying, even though he shouted for attention. Someone was always at a point in his experiment where there was no stopping. Apparatus had to be watched.

"But, Sister Jeremy," Mr. Simmons would plead, "I hate to disturb other classes, that is, lecture classes. And I can contact all the juniors and seniors in the laboratory at the same time."

"I understand, Mr. Simmons, but I disagree. Students like to be disturbed in lecture classes; it breaks the monotony. You're bound to get better attention. However, if you insist, I challenge you to get your point over in the laboratory."

So he would stride behind the instructor's desk, clear his throat blatantly and rap on the desk. No reaction! He even tried flicking the lights. Often Fred, the quarterback, would come to the rescue with, "Hey, you guys, Mr. Simmons wants to make an announcement." Even then he would get the attention of only a reluctant minority. The laboratory was a potpourri, but the future Curies and Pasteurs did not relish interruptions.

Once, on the very day of our fire extinguisher experiment, the coach was making an announcement to my preoccupied lab class. An absent-minded student inadvertently dropped a lighted match into a crock, which was chock-full of waste chemicals and paper. A blaze flared menacingly. The coach yelled, "Hold everything!" and dashed out. The boys reached for the fire extinguisher and put out the fire quickly and efficiently. We were all back at work when the coach rushed in and shouted, "Where's the fire?" He had run a block to the grade school corridor, the nearest place he remembered having seen a fire extinguisher.

The case of the fire extinguisher threatened to become my nemesis. Red and Pete, Jr., had recharged the generator for the second division the next day. This division was eager to have the fire demonstration, especially since news of the two previous incidents had spread. Fred and Eugenia were demonstrating. The basket had a substantial blaze, but not a drop of fluid would exude from the extinguisher. "Fake," whispered someone. How sorry I was that

I had been impatient with Pete, Sr., the day before; how I wished for him now! I was about to send for Red and Pete, Jr., when quick-witted Dorothy doused the flames with good old-fashioned H_2O. After the turmoil a small voice piped, "Sister Jeremy, we used the extinguisher last night and it was all right."

"Last night?" I exclaimed. "What were you doing in the laboratory last night, Ann?"

"We were practicing for the amateur program, Sister."

"Did you have a fire?"

"No, we used it for thunder. It made a swell noise when we rolled it on the floor. But it was so messy. All kinds of white watery stuff came out."

Again I had recourse to Sister Ida. "Sister Ida, do they have to use this laboratory for everything? It's hard enough keeping the place in order after the hundred students invade it to work their biweekly experiment, without cleaning up after a previous evening's dramatics, and last week's putrid flowers that someone has dumped into the laboratory crocks."

Sister Ida's gentle, penetrating eyes made me lower my own. I knew I had to supernaturalize these tiny trials, but it was good to hear her counsel. "Sister Jeremy, these circumstances can do much for you. Learning to work with others is one of the chief hardships and glories of religious life. Ask the Sisters to remind their students to be careful with the flowers. If you're there at the time, you can remind them yourself. The laboratory is the only place the ten high school classes have for water, but I realize that they ought to be more careful. This is part of our poverty bargain."

I did not have long to wait to try out Sister Ida's advice. One day as Red was helping me set up demonstration apparatus, in came Ann with a container of flowers headed for the sink.

"You're gonna get killed, Annie," Red warned.

I paid little attention to this typical boy-girl banter.

"Go away with you, Red. What for?"

"Who said you could go south with that graduate? It's the only liter one we have."

I glanced up and gasped. Our one and only liter graduate doubling as a vase? Ann was nonchalantly emptying the water. With dismay I saw that a sizable chip at the beak of the graduate climaxed a neat crack along its twelve-inch side. By this time I was at the sink. "Ann, did you take this graduate out of here?"

"Yes, Sister Jeremy."

"But don't you know this is lab property?"

"Yes, Sister, but it's always standing around empty, so I thought you didn't need it."

"Didn't need it—ohhh!" My frustration was reaching flood level.

"I'm sorry, Sister, truly I am." Ann was all contrition. "We . . . we just didn't have a vase tall enough for these long-stemmed flowers."

"Dames!" ejaculated Red.

"No interference, please," I ordered. "Now, Ann, you realize that the graduate is chipped and cracked and will have to be replaced, don't you?"

"Yes, of course, Sister, I'll be glad to pay for it," Ann agreed.

"And as for a vase for your May altar——"

But the temptation to interrupt was too much for Red. "You kids oughta buy a vase outa class dues—" he saw my displeasure for "interference" and concluded in a hasty mumble—"or somethin'."

Yes, this business of training faculty and students in the use of the laboratory-supply room was "part of our poverty bargain," as Sister Ida had said. More than once I secretly thanked the Lord it was poverty we had vowed and not *patience!* There's one virtue that's due for a deal of frazzling in a science teacher's life!

Poverty of space and convenience no doubt, but not poverty of training or professional spirit characterized the faculty of St. Albert's. School meetings of various kinds were a regular occurrence. Indeed, often a free day or a much-needed Saturday would be sacrificed to attend them. Educational magazines arrived at the convent monthly and were duly perused for new ideas and methods.

Students for the most part seemed to catch some of this zest for educational improvement. There is probably no better place for students to practice give-and-take than the laboratory, with its constant

44

rubbing of elbows by partners and neighbors. Here they develop patience, co-operation and a sense of humor.

Red, whose ambition was the medical field, realizing the necessity of a fundamental training in chemistry, had determined to master the subject, and had selected as his partner, Pete, Jr. I admired his generosity, thinking he intended to help the poor chap. During every laboratory period I saw Pete was more and more at the dispensing table and less and less at the laboratory place, while Red hardly ever moved. My suspicions were aroused. Was Pete making useless trips to fritter away his time? I determined to watch him, no easy task with forty students demanding attention at every stage of their activities, from wanting cleaning equipment to adjusting delicate instruments.

Students were never allowed to remove anything from the storage shelves. Chemicals for the day were always at the dispensing table. One day I missed Pete. He was not at his place with Red. I scanned the laboratory and finally located him in the rear of the room. Slowly and methodically, Pete was struggling over the names on the labels of chemicals on the storage shelves. "He could read names of chemicals at home from his text," I muttered to myself as I wove through the students toward him.

"What are you looking for?" I demanded impatiently when I reached his side.

"Diluted water, Sister," he answered worriedly.

I set my jaw. "Diluted water?"

He was very calm. "Red sent me for it. But it ain't on the table. Somebody must have swiped it."

Letting students choose their laboratory partners was approved psychological procedure; it was also an open door to "ulterior motives." Red, that Red, I mumbled to myself as I distractedly pondered the best way to direct him toward more thoughtfulness and unselfishness.

With a few exceptions like Pete I had some brilliant students in the years I spent at St. Albert's, most of them, from large families of middle-class income. Many of their parents, not fortunate enough to have had a formal education themselves, wanted to ensure such opportunities for their children. These parents had built and maintained this parochial school, sacrificing little luxuries and even necessities to preserve for their children the "Faith of their Fathers." Their children had inherited the characteristic energy of their parents.

Many of the students held a part-time job four to six hours a day besides carrying a full high school schedule. Yet their alertness was sometimes astonishing. On one occasion we were correcting a true-false examination in physics. I called on Hugo to explain a statement.

Hugo read, "The efficiency of the screw is high." He debated briefly.

Anton's snappy voice at his left quipped, "Oh, change 'screw' to 'Hugo' and write 'false'."

The students at St. Albert's took one another at face value.

The curriculum required all juniors to register for physics. Seniors had their choice between chemistry and bookkeeping. Traditionally, the two senior groups had dubbed each other "stinkers" and "pencil pushers." The classes usually ran parallel. During a lecture one day I was aware that the senior chemists were suspiciously attentive. The explanation followed closely on the heels of my thought. A rap at the door summoned me to a very disturbed bookkeeping instructor.

"Sister!" she gasped. "Your—your——" She choked and, holding her handkerchief tightly to her nose, pointed upward. But I did not have to look up, for the characteristic odor of hydrogen sulfide, best known as "rotten-egg gas," was pouring down from the "pencil pushers'" room above the laboratory. Into the fifty inkwells of these innocents the "stinkers" had stuffed iron sulfide! Reaction with the ink had done the rest.

I knew what I should do, but I anticipated trouble. I turned to the "chemikers." Already the guilty ones were coming toward me. "What do you want us to do, Sister Jeremy?" Anton asked. They had tasted victory worth any chastisement, and they gave themselves a just sentence. They collected, cleaned and refilled every inkwell.

I'm glad to say the spirit of American sportsmanship character-

46

ized these schooltime foes. In every game the umpire, whether parent, teacher or chum, received due respect. Each tried earnestly to fill his position while playing for the team. They were united in a loyal bond. Grief in one family was everyone's and so were their joys.

Despite the aversion of some of the students to science, they were constantly watching for opportunities to verify or, if possible, to nullify the instructor's statements. Pete, Jr., our "quiz kid," was one of these doubting souls. He was spending his fifth year in high school and his second in chemistry. One day I had explained the use of hydrogen fluoride gas in the etching of glass.

"You don't mean, Sister," he queried, scratching his blond thatch, "that a little gas can make marks on glass?"

Though unconvinced by my further explanation, he followed directions, worked with the class and prepared his piece of glass for etching. Time was required for the reaction; the setup had to be left undisturbed till the next day.

Early the next morning Pete was waiting for me at the laboratory door. He greeted me briefly and hurried to examine his etching. Soon I heard a low whistle, followed by, "Can I do my etching over, Sister?"

"Didn't yours turn out well, Pete?"

"Yes, Sister Jeremy," he said, "it's real good. But last night I was telling my girl about how I wrote her initials and mine in a heart on a piece of glass. I promised to give it to her if it worked."

"Talk sense, Pete. It worked so why do you want to do it over?"

Pete looked at his shoes, dug his toe into the floor, fumbling for words. "Well, Sister . . . well, Sister Jeremy," he struggled, "I—I didn't put her initials on it. Honest, Sister, I just told her that because I didn't think it was going to work."

This third year at St. Albert's I was appointed moderator of the senior class. Now I had to worry about things that were more important than teaching facts. My appointment involved the deeper part of education—molding character. This was the year that Red, Fred and Eugenia were seniors. Pete, Jr., had been reassigned as a junior.

In October of the year when Piccard and his gondola landed in

47

Cadiz, Ohio, the physics classes had seen the gondola on display. I was happy in their appreciation of the scientific, but I was not prepared to meet their ambition to imitate.

"If Piccard could make an eleven-mile ascent, why can't we, the science students of St. Albert's?" they reasoned.

I explained the hazard of such an attempt, but all to no avail. I had recourse to an illustration comparing the height of Mount Everest with that which the balloonist had reached. "At these altitudes the air is so rare," I emphasized, "that the lungs can't absorb enough oxygen to support life. And the air pressure is so low that the blood vessels burst."

"But," they said, unable to grasp the effects of unevenness of pressure, "if there is no air, how can blood vessels burst? Can you prove it, Sister?"

This was Thursday. The next laboratory period would be Tuesday. "Class," I said, "if one of you can bring a gallon tin can with a lid that can be suitably sealed, I will demonstrate the effect of atmospheric differences on partially evacuated vessels." This privilege I granted to the three classes in physics, totaling about one hundred twenty students.

As one of the classes was leaving the laboratory, I heard Pete say, "Do we look so dumb, or is Sister just trying to get us off the track?"

Before eight o'clock the following Tuesday, I was at my desk in the senior bungalow. A shadow fell across the desk and I turned to see Sister Basil looking as though there were murder in the laboratory.

"*Sister Mary Jeremy*," she demanded, "what are you going to do today?"

What was I going to do today? The faculty often wondered if Sister Basil in her efficiency did not have complete records of our future thoughts, words and deeds. Why this sudden bafflement on her part?

"Why, Sister, I . . ."

But some muffled noise drew my attention toward the court, and Sister Basil was asking, "Can you explain this?"

Outside the laboratory door stood one hundred twenty physics

48

students, each holding a one-gallon can. I felt as though I were in "Hilarity Hall" in an amusement park. Everything was in a whirl. I hoped that the next time the laboratory came around, I could grab it.

"Sister Jeremy!" There was a sympathetic note in Sister Basil's voice. It restored my equilibrium. "What I mean is, what kind of experiment is on the agenda?"

"Sister," I said, "we are going to demonstrate the effects of atmospheric pressure. Would you like to come?"

Sister came. I opened the series of experiments by driving air out of a can with steam formation, then sealing the can. Then I allowed a little cold water to flow over the can. It folded up like a fan. The students gasped. I gave the signal and the forty students of that division crushed their cans. Three physics classes that day, six periods, one hundred twenty crushed cans. The principal's interest never lagged. She paid us intermittent visits the whole day long.

At supper that evening, I found two boxes of candy bars with a note:

To thank you for the nice time today. This is for you and your your fellow Sisters. Hope you all enjoy it. Sister Basil.

Chapter Three

"Go 'way, my fine feathered friend," I grumbled, pulling the pillow over my head. But the cardinal, from his tree perch outside my window, persisted.

"C'mere! C'mere! C'mere!"

I raised my head to get a view of him. The sleeping porch, which jutted out from the second floor, proved an ideal place from which to imbibe this experience called "spring morning." The redbud was radiant. My cardinal in his new spring suit was hardly discernible among its branches. Every tree and bush had felt the touch of God's hand and was a miracle of newborn leaves and buds. The air, too, had a newness about it. Once more Mr. Cardinal attracted my attention, and by now I welcomed his chanted invitation although there were still ten minutes before rising time. It would not be long before our return to Tannerton for the summer. The thought heightened the spring morning's joy.

Everything, in the succeeding days, pointed to spring and vacation. The hundred goldfish that I had tended all winter in the laboratory aquaria were now in the outdoor pond. The Glee Club practiced incessantly for the spring concert. Sister Martin's First Communion class passed and repassed through the court on its way to practice for the big day. My chemistry students, taking their final examinations, reacted characteristically. Red designed inkblots on his paper; Ann chewed her pencil; Eugenia gazed intelligently into space; Pete, Jr., tried to borrow answers. As the test progressed, I wandered to the window to watch a bird build its nest in a near-by sycamore tree. Sister Basil was coming toward the classroom, a large envelope in her hand. That could mean only one thing—summer appointments—another oasis in our teaching career. No matter how drab or exclusive, how ordinary or exciting, the private school where we Sisters labored from September to June, we all welcomed the summer change. We had experienced that a change in occupation was truly a vacation. This was to be my third summer back to Tannerton for the annual week of retreat. The remaining weeks of summer held varied schedules and diversified employments for each of us.

There was always the element of chance, however, in summer appointments. In accord with its educational program, the community conducts several private institutions: one for adolescent girls with special problems, "The Farm" for retarded children and St. Michael's Home for orphaned and homeless ones. At these places a twelve-month personnel is necessary. To afford the regular staff opportunity for retreat, summer school, a little relaxation or a much-needed rest, other members of the community are appointed to substitute in the June-to-September interval.

The week allotted to each of us for retreat was well planned. It was a time set apart to withdraw from the daily grind, from everything and everyone. We placed ourselves completely in God's presence. Our spiritual progress in the state we had freely chosen called for careful scrutiny. Had we grown in the love of God? That was the most important question. Were we more than ever united to God's Holy Will? That answer was the measure of the first. We determined to be good soldiers in this army of Christ, soldiers, physically, morally and spiritually fit to carry on the mammoth undertaking of Christian education. Under the direction of a Franciscan priest, we looked back into the past year. Four one-hour conferences daily aided in evaluating our duties as religious teachers, duties to ourselves, to our fellow religious and to the children placed under our care. With Christ our Captain, Who would guide and strengthen us in the days to come, we planned our campaign for the next year against the world, the flesh and the devil.

When retreat ended, we would disperse. The majority of us usually spent the summer in school as the teacher, the taught or both at our own Padua College in Tannerton. Others would attend various universities.

Though there were only these few places where we might be assigned, our interest in appointments always ran high.

"Children," I heard Sister Martin say as her class neared the bungalow, "show Sister Jeremy how beautifully you keep rank, in straight lines, like soldiers." Sister Martin's large dark eyes flashed with excitement when I met her at the door that last day at dismissal. "You're going to make first retreat," she exclaimed, "and go to summer school at the college! So'm I!"

The chance element made it like playing bunco—the way we play it in the convent—that is, a gamble whose outcome does not lessen our fascination but rather satisfies our curiosity. Noontime brought as much excitement as any political convention ever aroused. Lobbying in the kitchen was at a high that day, until Sister Marie shooed us out with, "You're a flock of magpies!"

Sister Marie had taken care of an invalid matron before entering the convent and sometimes found our youthful exuberance rather trying. She never consulted the Tannerton appointments, since she had always been assigned the second retreat.

Sister Ida, sitting opposite Sister Marie at table, suddenly remarked enthusiastically, "You're going to like it at the Farm."

"Yes," Sister Marie replied abstractedly as she reached for her salad. Then her arm stopped in mid-air. "What did you say?" she gasped. "Who's going to the Farm?"

"Didn't you read the list?" Sister Ida asked in surprise. "You're to go to the Farm the day after graduation."

Sister Marie sputtered like an outboard motor! "But . . . but . . . but . . . I can't! I have to can the cherries. And I ordered two crates of berries for Monday. And the rhubarb is just ready to be picked!"

We were agape at this high frequency so foreign to Sister Marie. But she continued: "And the pantry needs cleaning; besides both of my habits need mending and cleaning and I still have to sew my new coifs."

All of us collaborated to get Sister Marie ready. Her leaving would rend the family group. Knowing that the same personnel would not comprise St. Albert's again, we became more appreciative of each other. Especially were we more attentive to the wants of dear old Sister Bonaventure, who had served as housekeeper at St. Albert's for thirty-seven years. We all loved this sweet-tempered nun whose eyes still held the sparkle of youth. We doted on Sister Bonaventure. This was to be her last trip from St. Albert's. This year marked the fiftieth anniversary of her profession. The day of the closing of first retreat she would celebrate her Golden Jubilee. Reverend Mother had already promised her an easier occupation at the mother house in Tannerton, and we knew we would miss her unselfish devotion.

Often after starting our school day one of us would discover that we had forgotten something. Sister Bonaventure was "Old Reliable" in finding any article and graciously giving it to the student whom we had sent for it. Our apology to her after classes would always receive the same answer, "That was a pleasure, Sister."

After school we would gather around in the kitchen and relate the day's highlights. "Take some more hot coffee. And spread yourself another piece of jelly bread," Sister Bonaventure would say, appreciating our anecdotes. "You must be hungry after working with those live wires."

"Ice cube?" I heard Sister Martin ask as I approached the kitchen for my after-school lunch one day late in May. That can't be Sister Basil and Sister Ida home from the diocesan meeting so soon, I thought. But sure enough, Sister Martin was serving them ice-cold lemonade. They looked tired and wilted.

"How's come so early?" I asked, joining them. "Business slow?"

"Monsignor cut the meeting short because of the extreme heat," Sister Basil informed us. "He's sending a notice about matters which he thought would be self-explanatory."

"It sure is hot," sighed Sister Martin, mopping her brow beneath the band.

"That reminds me." Sister Ida smiled. "While we were waiting for the bus some ladies in sun dresses went by. One of them took a look at us and said, 'Good grief! Why don't they put *more* clothes on?' "

"You should have told her you were doing penance for the slack slacks and short shorts," laughed Sister Martin.

Sister Basil paused in her sipping. "Some things, Sister Martin, are best left unsaid. Any business while we were gone, Sister Bonaventure?"

"Yes, Sister Basil, Sister Marie jotted it all down."

Sister Marie popped in from the porch and took several slips of paper from her apron pocket. "Here it is, Sister. First, the caps and gowns came. They're in the school office. Here's the signed slip."

"They are so late this year we'll barely have time to check and see if all the measurements are right," said Sister Ida, rinsing out her glass.

"Do that first thing in the morning, Sister. What else, Sister Marie?" Sister Basil took the cap and gown receipt and folded it.

"The florist called and wants to know what kind of flowers and how many bouquets you want for the altar for graduation. Then, some man at the *Clarion* called for pictures of the graduates and a list of special honors." Sister Marie took a deep breath. "Yes, and a Mrs. Wencel wanted to know if her Johnnie is going to pass and if not what should she do with him. And Mrs. Olcovy called to say that Gertie is over the chicken pox and can she come in for her tests next week?"

Sister Basil was jotting in her little pocket pad. "Goodness, Sister Marie! It's a wonder you could get anything done between the door and the phone."

Sister Marie chuckled good-naturedly. "Oh, I'm used to it. But today *was* a little busier than usual."

"It's the end-of-the-year rush," mused Sister Martin between bites of cooky. "You know, these graduates are my first second graders at St. Albert's. Why, I can still see them in their First Communion outfits."

"Look who's getting misty-eyed!" I teased. "But say, you mean I've been teaching your products? No wonder I've been having a time of it!"

Sister Martin gave the air an innocuous punch in my direction.

55

"Come on now, Simon Legree! They're the best you'll ever have; admit it!"

"Oh, I wouldn't say that!" I parried.

"Never mind, Sister Jeremy, you'll be sorry when I'm transferred from St. Albert's." Sister Martin elongated her face in a mock doleful expression that made me laugh outright. And Sister Bonaventure joined in. "Honestly, Sister Basil, these two young ones! I'm going to miss their joshing around. They do more arguing, and yet get along quite well, I would say."

"That is a charitable interpretation, Sister," commended Sister Basil, looking over her glasses with something of a twinkle. And then to me: "Sister Jeremy, I expect everything in perfect order in the lab and all the school storage labeled and properly inventoried before June eighteenth."

"Yes, Sister Basil."

"And, Sister Martin, I'm depending on you for the grade school inventory. You've been here long enough to take the responsibility." She paused in the doorway. "Thanks for the lemonade."

"Yes, Sister Basil." Sister Martin jumped up and did a rapid pivot, her eyes dancing. "Just think! One week till graduation and two weeks till we go home to Tannerton! Happy day!"

Ten minutes before rising time on June 18, my cardinal, faithful to his self-imposed duty, awakened me with a different song: "Hurry! Hurry! Hurry!"

"You're right," I mused, half aloud. There were many things to be done, this day of departure for Tannerton. At the signal for rising I answered, *Deo gratias,* to Sister Martin's murmured, *"Benedicamus Domino."*

"Thanks be to God for you," I said to the cardinal under my breath, "and for Red, and Fred, and Pete, Jr., and Eugenia, and Pete, Sr.," I added as I caught sight of the last-named plodding toward church.

The next twenty minutes flew. I tried to meditate on the religious clothing, cord, crucifix and veil, as I put them on, saying the customary prayers for grace to remember their significance, a hidden life of prayer and mortification, in union with a crucified God.

In the chapel my own unconventional prayers confused my usual community exercises. "Lord," I prayed, "Thank You for this year at St. Albert's." A few unpleasant incidents had but served to enrich my memory of many happy days. I had learned to walk in the shadow as well as the sunlight.

The signal for the conclusion of meditation interrupted my reverie. "Thank You, Lord, for the grace of this meditation," I prayed quickly before starting over to the parish church for Holy Mass, the consummation of our morning offering and the pivot of our daily activities.

Each action this last day before leaving was a mixture of intensified attachments for St. Albert's and eager longing for Tannerton.

The traditional farewell meal was set for ten that night. Those who were not leaving for Tannerton on the midnight train outdid themselves in the culinary art. The travelers were served in great style—Deshler-Wallick and Palmer House were outstripped because the homey atmosphere of St. Albert's was added to that of superior service.

The trip in the chartered Pennsy was pleasant. We chatted, prayed, slept and dreamed of meeting old associates, classmates and friends. Although no one voiced her sentiments, a decided lull disclosed our universal expectancy as we neared our destination.

So again for the third summer Sister Olivia, my classmate and novitiate partner, was waiting to greet me. I was delighted to hear her familiar voice as I set down my suitcase in the main hall outside the Superior's office.

"It's about time you Easterners are in," she said with her eager smile. "We thought you were flooded."

"Why, why, Sister Olivia," I exclaimed, turning her toward the light from the doorway, "what's wrong? You look worn out; are you ill?"

"Last minute preparations always wear me out. I'll be all right in a few days." And she smiled more broadly. That smile lent beauty to her rather large, plain features. The strain of teaching for the past three years had not disturbed her calm serenity, but she was pale and apparently exhausted. Some five inches taller than I, she looked down at me with quiet dignity and friendliness. How fortunate I was to have this loyal friend, so dependable, conscientious and unassuming! I resolved to coax her into an extra glass of milk daily to help build her up.

I remember how Sister Olivia and I as girls had traded oranges for cake in our lunch boxes, how I had worked her arithmetic and algebra problems and how she had translated my French. She had lost her mother in infancy, so I had always shared my mom with her. She reciprocated by inspiring me with a devotion to the Mother of God, a deep devotion which she had learned from her father who realized a child's need for a mother.

There was so much that home-coming to tell each other before retreat opened at eight that evening. The six days of retreat we spent in silence among hundreds of Sisters. But sharing the same experience could now as always deepen the silent understanding between us.

Our rank in the religious community according to the date of our entrance brought us next to each other in chapel, in the refectory, at conferences and in the dormitory. I probably would have succumbed to the temptation of relating some anecdote had not Sister Olivia's self-control inspired me. I longed to be like her. We kept retreat conscientiously and celebrated Jubilee Day, the traditional close of the annual first retreat with great festivity.

That year, my ninth of religious profession, five Sisters had reached their fiftieth anniversary and we were as one in celebrating their Golden Jubilee. The day was a round of activities—long beautiful chapel ceremonies, serving and entertaining guests, and an evening program in the auditorium.

"Hurry, Sister Jeremy," Sister Olivia reminded me immediately after breakfast. "We'll be late for choir."

"I'll be there as soon as I put these meat platters in the steamer. They must be piping hot for dinner. With five jubilarians there will be hundreds of guests. Oops, I almost dropped that stack on the floor."

When we reached the chapel, the jubilee procession had already formed. We slipped through a side entrance to the choir and breathlessly chimed in on the opening bar of "*Jubilate Deo*." At slight intervals we caught sight of the ceremony—"Thou shalt sanctify the fiftieth year . . . for it is the year of jubilee." For fifty years the five celebrants had observed "these things"—fifty years of poverty, chastity and obedience. "All the days of my life" had passed, for them, beyond calculation, though my mathematical mind was tempted to work out the multiplication. I remembered that our divine Master was above the precise payment of strict justice. He had promised an eternity of joy for a few years of loving service—and besides that, "a hundredfold in this life." Today's solemnity was a partial fulfillment of that promise of a hundredfold.

The days of reception and profession were days of expectation, but this day of jubilee was one of triumph. The tones of the *Jubilate Deo* merged into the suppliant Kyrie eleison of the Mass of Thanksgiving. The determined and dignified bearing of the jubilarians as they neared the altar to renew their vows made us suddenly realize that it had been fifty years since they first pronounced these words in public. Now in the evening of their lives they proved just as generous and even more loving in their threefold dedication. As we drank in the significance of the ceremony, our admiration for these five loyal nuns grew, and slowly the wondering thought took root that we creatures should dare to offer to God the things that are not really ours—ourselves, our time, our talents—everything. From all eternity His, yet we asked Him to accept them as gifts. Suddenly we knew that there was only one way that we could be donors to God. That was by love, the love of God which is perfection. To vow such seemingly impossible things in the midst of wealth, with our weak human nature, our wills so wayward, would be foolhardy without the divine catalyst of God's grace, always given in abundance to a generous heart. The Choir's "*Te Deum*" confirmed our mutual participation with the celebrants. The final verse resounded through the chapel: "In Thee, O Lord, I have hoped, I shall not be confounded in eternity."

We from St. Albert's watched with loving eyes as Sister Bonaventure, crowned with a golden wreath, walked, a little falteringly, out of the chapel. She was sixty-eight years old. Her mother, still active at eighty-five, was present for the ceremony together with Sister's six brothers, their wives, five sisters, their husbands, children and grandchildren. A festive reception on the campus followed the chapel ceremony. The fourteen acres were covered with friends, relatives, clergy and religious. I was lost in the land of fancy with some of Sister Bonaventure's grandnieces and grandnephews when a slight tap on the shoulder brought me back to a workaday world.

"Sister Jeremy," Sister Olivia was saying, "did you forget we're serving the guests today?"

I crossed the campus more quickly than religious decorum and the admonitions of my novice mistress would have recommended. I jerked my apron from the hook and stood ready for service. Sister Olivia was still some distance behind. I noticed anew how exhausted she seemed. "You're not feeling good today, are you?" I asked as we pushed a cart of ham platters into the first dining room.

"Just the same old headache. It'll go away."

But it didn't go away, and the day was clouded for me by anxiety for Sister Olivia. I finally made her promise to ask for an appointment with the eye doctor.

One of the features of the evening's get-together in the auditorium was reminiscences of the jubilarians. The stage was neatly arranged with flowers and easy chairs for the jubilarians and Mother Regina. Sister Colette was called on first to give an account of her work at St. Michael's Home. She had practically grown up with the institution.

The present location with its one hundred acres was the third Home in fifty years. Some twenty years earlier our religious community had responded to the plea of Tannerton to care for its homeless and destitute children by placing needy girls with the academy resident students. But what happened to the homeless boys? There was no institution for them in the vicinity. An old farmhouse on the grounds of the present college campus was converted into the first Home. The initial enrollment consisted of two girls and one boy. In one year the house was bulging with eighteen children, and there was a waiting list of about fifty. It was necessary to move to a larger home a few blocks away. Another move soon followed to the present yellow brick structure a mile out of Tannerton, which houses one hundred and sixty children. Sister Colette estimated that about eighteen hundred children had been cared for under her direction at the Home. We knew from her story, unlike the "Old Woman Who Lived in a Shoe," she knew just what to do. She had converted an institution into St. Michael's Home.

Applause followed applause. One corner of the auditorium was especially responsive, for there was assembled a group of Sisters who had come under Sister Colette's guidance as orphaned children and following her example had joined the ranks.

"Thank you, Sister Colette," Mother Regina commended. "You have lived a full life. May God always bless you.

"Sisters," Mother Regina continued, "we also have with us today a jubilarian who has spent thirty-seven years at our Indian Reservation School in Wisconsin. She's the only member of our community whom Uncle Sam remembers monthly with a check, her pension. May I introduce Sister Germaine?"

Stepping to the front of the stage Sister Germaine curtsied to Mother Regina, then to us. Again applause. The northern Wisconsin winters had coppered her skin with a healthful glow. She was tall and erect, with a mischievous smile playing around her mouth and her small oval eyes.

"Mother Regina wants me to tell something about the contrasting conditions of our Pinefield School today and yesterday, the yesterday of fifty years ago!" She whispered the last phrase through her cupped hands, looking slyly toward Mother Regina, as if she did not know this span of time. "Where was I? Oh, yes, Mother wants to know about the work. Work? I suppose we did have plenty to keep our minds off ourselves." Then she leaned forward and in a stage whisper, as if Mother Regina again were not in on this, said, "That's the biggest secret—keep your mind off yourself." Drawing back she continued. "Twenty-four hours a day, eleven months of the year, we had the girls with us. We lived in a three-story building facing Chequamegon Bay. The substantial building

61

was some thirty by sixty feet. Each room had a small stove for burning logs. With this we managed some comfort in forty below zero weather. On pleasant days the girls helped stack wood in the shed. Daily the various rooms were supplied with neat piles of logs by the particular girls assigned to each. Bathing facilities, like so many other things, were primitive. The girls used a washtub set up in the kitchen. The water was heated on the large kitchen range. Today there is a central heating system and, of course, bathrooms. The daily routine of training the girls for family living—sewing, cooking, washing, caring for the home—and all domestic duties were added to those of the classroom. But now the girls no longer live there. Since last June it has been a day school for boys and girls, whose parents bring them in a car if they live too far to walk to school.

"What I would like most to tell you is a highlight of forty years ago. At the time we still had a day school at Washburn and one at Green Cliff. On every favorable Saturday from May to October, the Sisters from these places visited us. How we looked forward to these visits! Being just a handful and so far from Tannerton, we delighted in the sight of the familiar Franciscan habit. The Sisters from Green Cliff trekked the three miles through the dense woods, and the Washburners cut the ten miles across the bay on Mr. Olson's ferry, the *Scater*. Mr. Olson, a kindly man, toted the Sisters back and forth every Saturday, gratis. When the Sisters said that they did not think they ought to take advantage of him like this, he always replied, 'Happy to do it, Sister Ladies.'

"I don't know how happy he was the day Lake Superior was too rough to bring the *Scater* to shore in the bay. Watching from our school door, we could see the waves bouncing good *Scater* all over the bay. We were sad thinking that the Sisters would have to go back to Washburn without visiting us. But big-hearted Mr. Olson knew how to solve the problem. He lowered a rowboat from the ferry. One of the men stepped in and the other two from the ferry carefully helped the three Sisters, one at a time, into the boat, and rowed them to shore. Beautiful Chequamegon Bay!" And her eyes looked beyond us over the expanse of five hundred miles. "The picturesqueness of the *Scater* has been supplanted by a bus making three round trips daily. . . . In closing, may I ask all of you to do two things to ensure a fuller life in the convent? Love your work and love to be with the members of our community. I thank you." She curtsied and made her way back to her place.

And so the evening passed in recounting simple joys. Others had had no less colorful experiences in their fifty years as religious. Sister Felicia had seen varied fields of labor, while Sister Alcuin had spent almost her entire religious life, if not at one place, at least in one field. She was, God bless her, a music teacher.

Sister Bonaventure emphasized the good she had always found in all the Sisters with whom she lived during her religious life. We were chagrined at not being worthy of her, but appreciative of her words. We left the auditorium loving her more than ever before, and sad, too, for having muffed our chances of imitating her virtues more closely. We knew that next year Sister would be stationed at the mother house in Tannerton.

"Now tell me, does this wonderful day have to include a summer school schedule?" asked Sister Olivia as a group of us stopped before the bulletin board outside the auditorium shortly before retiring.

"You might as well come down to earth," I told her. "Face facts. Tomorrow we register for the summer session. You'd better carry a light schedule," I advised. "You look less rested than when you came in for retreat. And remember, drink that daily quart of milk Mother Regina prescribed."

"You're always facing facts, Sister Jeremy." Sister Olivia ignored my concern. "Don't facts get monotonous?"

However, Sister Olivia agreed that summer school at Padua College was refreshing. Just to slip one's feet under the desk on the other side of the track and be a student again was a vacation in itself. We always left with new ideas and resolutions for the coming scholastic year.

I felt that science at St. Albert's would be different after this summer. Besides teaching a class of postulants, I was to take a course called "Trends in the Teaching of Science." The trends came in large doses—what to do when there was a shortage of equipment, space, time and the like. When I brought up the situation of St. Albert's laboratory being used as a general store, the Sisters from elite high schools and academies gasped in holy horror.

"Well," I defended, "St. Albert's has a homey atmosphere." My audience wanted to snicker, but courtesy prevented them.

The most relaxing hour of any summer session is the evening recreation. Sometimes we rounded up a pinochle game or played a few hands of bridge or five hundred. At other times we arranged benches in large circles on the lawn and told yarns. Many of the Sisters had lived together at the same mission, in the novitiate or at previous summer sessions. Thus we came to know many of our seven hundred Sisters.

What we called the St. Albert's summer group consisted of the Sisters who had been or were now stationed there. Those who were no longer at St. Albert's were curious about all the Johnnies and Susies, their brothers and sisters, and Pete the janitor's progress in getting under the faculty's feet. One particular summer Sister Basil was at Tannerton with us and we would get her into our outdoor ring and tease her about her magisterial performances of the previous year. Her sportsmanship being superb, she would enjoy these incidents with us. But she had methods of retaliation.

"Sister Jeremy," Sister Basil once asked before our large circle, "do you remember the first time the Reverend Mother came to visit your class?"

"Yes," Sister Bonaventure interrupted, "I remember that, for I never saw Sister Jeremy's shoes shined so well. She always said highly polished shoes were too rich a diet for chemicals."

"And," continued Sister Basil, "as I walked into Sister Jeremy's class with Reverend Mother, I happened to glance at those highly polished shoes. So did Reverend Mother. But then she scanned me quizzically. One shoe was like a set of reflecting mirrors; the other, which had never been a mate in shape or size, was practically out at the toes and gray."

One evening that memorable summer we were agreeably surprised by a visit from Fred and Eugenia, the famous couple of the oxygen experiment. They were on their honeymoon. We could never conjecture for which couple from St. Albert's the wedding bells would ring next. Often those who were constantly at swords' ends in class would pledge loyalty until death did them part.

Fred told about the time that Sister Ida had kept him and Red, our famous linguist, after school. They were to report in the laboratory. They decided on a practical joke and crept under her laboratory desk. Sister Ida noticed a slight movement as she walked into the laboratory but said nothing. Eugenia was arranging apparatus. Sister Ida said rather casually, "Eugenia, Fred and Red were to report here after school. If you see them on the grounds, kindly tell them, since I have a good hour's work here, I'll wait for them."

"To our dismay—" Fred laughed—"Sister Ida took the laboratory notebooks to her desk and established herself custodian of our dugout. She almost put her foot in my mouth," he added. "We were cooped up and practically smothered to death."

"Yes, I was petrified," chimed in Eugenia. "I snailed along with the cleaning, hoping to see the outcome. I couldn't determine whether or not Sister Ida knew of their whereabouts. When I finally finished and bade Sister good-by, there was a strange twinkle in her eye."

"Twinkle?" exclaimed Fred. "There should have been! After we had crouched for a torturous hour, our M.P. went off duty with the words: 'Boys, you may leave now.'"

Another time the stories shifted to the present summer school kitchen. That noon Sister Marie had filled fifteen gravy boats. She called me to carry them to the Sisters' dining room.

"Sister Jeremy," she advised, "please make two trips."

"Just watch this, Sister Marie," I said, as I piled the boats on the tray. "I have this down to a system." I waved at her with my right hand, balancing the tray on my left. I backed into the swinging door, pivoted and cleared the second door. The portress, Sister Jane, had just delivered a message and was leaving the refectory. Suddenly a clatter of china disturbed the community spiritual reading.

"Oh, pardon me, Sister Jane," I gasped. "I'm so sorry."

"It's all right, Sister Jeremy," she said softly through the gravy,

65

looking like a Christmas figure candle which had been burning down for hours. All eyes were on us; no one had ears for the reader who, according to community custom, kept on reading.

It was a typical Tannerton summer. Each day the mercury climbed a little higher. Cicadas screeched all night: "Hotter tomorrow." One particularly hot night I alternately tossed and dozed. Suddenly something roused me. For a moment I thought someone had called. I listened but could hear only the cicadas. Not a leaf stirred on the maples and oaks which reached far above the dormitory windows. The clock in the tower struck one. I argued with myself. "Look, you have to rise at five. Get some sleep. You can't nod approval to the professor again tomorrow."

"Sister Jeremy!" The call was more distinct now. "Sister Jeremy." It was Sister Olivia's voice.

I slipped quietly over to her cell. "Did you call me, Sister?"

"Sister Jeremy," she moaned weakly.

Only the moon gave visibility. I felt her forehead. It was hot. I hurried down the corridor and woke Mother Regina. She saw at once that Sister Olivia was seriously ill. Within half an hour my best friend was in an ambulance on the way to St. Roch's Hospital.

"You go to bed, Sister Jeremy," Mother Regina advised as I pleaded to ride along.

Sister Olivia's look begged me to make this sacrifice of obedience willingly. "Pray for me, Sister Jeremy," she breathed.

I pressed her hand and whispered, "I will. You know I will. God keep you."

In the few days that followed we learned the cause of those persistent headaches. It was not eyestrain but a brain tumor, and it was inoperable. At the end of the week I decided to ask permission to visit Sister Olivia. The next day was Saturday. That morning I seemed to detect a strange sound in the five o'clock rising bell. I listened intently, hoping an unskilled novice had just tipped it. But soon my fears were confirmed. The bell was definitely tolling. I chilled; a cold clamminess came over me. It just couldn't be true.

Perhaps one of the older and infirm Sisters had gone to eternity during the night. I dressed and hurried to the chapel. The Sister leading the community prayers began: "In the name of the Father, and of the Son, and of the Holy Spirit. Amen. For our departed Sister Olivia." Tears rushed to my eyes and I could hardly see the tabernacle. The reality gradually dawned with the words "impossible, incredible" dinning in my ears. It simply couldn't be. But it was. Sister Olivia was dead. She who had been my lodestone to Christ, exhaustless in persuasion and encouragement, who with universal kindness spent her days in a labor of love, had gone where Charity lives eternally.

After Mass I learned the details. It was a beautiful death. The priest was there and Sister Olivia went to God smiling.

For eight days after a Sister's death we offer all our prayers and works for her as our tribute, our flowers for the Bride of Christ. In my round of duties those days I whispered continuous prayers that my beloved friend would soon come face to face with her Spouse.

I prayed that our childhood friendship had never lessened our love for Him to Whom we had vowed our lives. At times I was selfishly sad. Everything on the fourteen acres was a reminder. I was lonely when I walked alone or with a group on the paths where we had chatted and laughed and planned.

The two remaining weeks of summer school passed slowly.

The day ushering in the last week of the summer session was most welcome. It always caused hubbub, breaking the strain of cramming for finals. We dubbed it "Colored Envelope Day"—Mother Regina's clearinghouse. And today was a beautiful "Colored Envelope Day." Although most of the appointments for the summer were made in June, there were unavoidable circumstances which required readjustments. It was like small-town talk about who got a special delivery, telegram or air mail letter. At various places in the dining rooms colored envelopes containing new temporary appointments appeared.

And there at my place I spied a lovely pink envelope. I could hardly wait for spiritual reading to end to open it. Mother Regina was so thoughtful. How well she knew I needed a change to recover from my loss.

> Sister Jeremy, St. Michael's Home, until August 12. Try to leave as soon as examinations are over. Sister Colette and Sister Liguori, the superintendent, are anxious to leave for home visits.
>
> Devotedly,
> MOTHER MARY REGINA, O.S.F.
Superior General.

She surely was a queen. I had always wanted a try at the Home. There would be a hundred acres to roam around in with a group of youngsters before returning to St. Albert's. Returning? Who knew?

Chapter Four

Facing the state highway, on the northwest corner of a one-hundred-sixty-acre farm, is St. Michael's Home, a four-story, H-shaped, tan brick structure. The north wing runs parallel with Theodore Road. I had often been there, escorting visitors or benefactors through the building and grounds. The north wing is reserved for the boys; the south for the girls. The ground floor contains the playrooms, baths, kitchen and dining rooms for the one hundred sixty children and twenty Sisters. The offices and kindergarten are in the middle wing of the main floor; the chaplain's quarters are in the north wing and accommodations for the Sisters are provided in the south wing. On the third floor classrooms and infirmary are located; on the fourth, the chapel and dormitories.

Sister Liguori, superintendent of the Home, beamed and shook my hand warmly as I presented myself at the general office on August 3. "Sister Jeremy! What a relief to know you've arrived. You're our housemother for the small boys. Now Sister Colette and I can leave without any worries."

I rummaged through my mind as my imagination flashed all sorts of pictures before me. Small boys—six to ten years old—thirty-five of them. I had jogtrotted to classes of high school boys—with them, one could reason, but what chances had I here?

My eyes must have betrayed me. Sister Liguori encouraged me. "Now don't be crossing bridges before you come to them. You'll get along."

Her eyes told of dauntless zeal. She was middle-aged, about five feet four inches tall and well-proportioned. There were tired lines in her face but her charming hospitality convinced me of my new privilege to do things for others. Her years at the Home had deepened her broad and sympathetic understanding of human needs and problems. I had heard that a family spirit flourished in the midst of institutional living. Now I was to see for myself.

Sister Liguori explained as she took me into her office, "Sister Amabilis is housemother of the older boys. She'll take over my duties during my absence. Go to her with any problem. She'll help you."

"Did you send for me, Sister Liguori?" I heard from the doorway a few minutes later. "Oh, greetings, Sister Jeremy." And I turned to see Sister Amabilis, one of my novitiate classmates.

"Come in, Sister. You must have angels' intuition. How do you think Sister Jeremy will work out as housemother?" Sister Liguori asked with a twinkle in her eye.

My capabilities! Mentally, I was almost over the bridge. Already the thought of six-year-old squirmers gave me a roller-coaster feeling. Visions of seven-year-old paper-pellet shooters, eight-year-old water-gun masters, nine-year-old pranksters and ten-year-old whippersnappers rose up to dismay me.

Sister Amabilis joined in the fun. "Sister Jeremy and I have not been together since we left the novitiate almost ten years ago, but if she's true to form she'll probably ruin the entire Home shortly. What else can we do but accept the inevitable in the present emergency?"

This was my teasing welcome from Sister Amabilis. She reminded me of Sister Olivia in many ways—her repartee, her poise, her calmness. She was my senior in religion by two years. I knew her only from the few occasions when novices' and postulants' duties had brought us together. Her actions were slow, deliberate, well planned.

"Sister Jeremy," Sister Liguori said, turning to me, "Sister Colette is anxious to pack; would you mind going on duty immediately? The boys are at supper now. Leave your luggage here. I'll send it to the housemother's room adjoining the small boys' dormitory."

"Just let me get my apron from the case, Sister Liguori, and I'll be tripping along with Sister Amabilis," I agreed heartily, finally catching some of her enthusiastic Home spirit.

On the way to the boys' quarters, Sister Amabilis briefed me swiftly and clearly. "Transient children are our biggest problem.

Frequent changing of companions is not good for their morale. Many come from broken homes, with no respect for parents or for their sisters and brothers; from homes with little, if any, training in courtesy, deference, etiquette. Others here are true orphans— many have known a beautiful home life. They have lost devoted and loving parents through death. The Sisters try to instill into all the children a love for Christian home life."

We stood now in the doorway of the small boys' dining room. "Here we are. I'll be on my way now. Sister Colette will put her charges into your care very shortly."

The boys had just finished eating their supper. I watched two boys whom Sister Colette addressed as Rudy and Marcellus clear tables and stack dishes. The smaller ones folded the napkins neatly and passed them to the lad at the end of the table, who in turn put them in the buffet. They were oblivious of me, to them a casual visitor; they seemed unafraid—probably brimful of mischief. At a sign from Sister Colette they stood and said grace. Then Sister Colette smilingly nodded to me saying, "Boys, this is Sister Jeremy. She will be your housemother while I'm gone."

They scanned me with evident misgivings. "Good evening, Sister," they chorused heartily enough.

I knew that I could never be to them what the small, plump, blue-eyed Sister Colette was. Her warm, understanding heart permeated all her actions, her every word. She loved these homeless youngsters. I knew little about this phase of our community's social work. Now it was my duty to blend theory with love and see how practical I could prove myself.

Thirty-five small boys! I was sure there were thirty-five hundred, what with so many vivacious bodies pushing toward me, pulling on my habit and veil, stepping on my feet, elbowing one another to get closer. In the commotion I had not noticed Sister Colette leave. I was cornered in the dining room. The heat of Tannerton's summer and the smell of food momentarily nauseated me. I grappled with my memory. There was a playground somewhere. I tried to catch enough breath to suggest, "Boys, how about playing outdoors?"

"Oh, yes, Sister Jeremy, we always do after supper," someone

71

answered. But no one moved. Now what to do? All my cards were shuffled but not a trump in my hand. Then I remembered—this was to be solitaire. I wondered how many cards I would have on the board at the end of the week.

I tried again. "How about going outdoors to play?" I gasped audibly. A sudden rush broke against me with such lusty shouts as, "Hey, you guys, quit shoving." "Get going, will you?" "Gee, we want to go with Sister Jeremy." "Well, so do we."

I almost stepped on them a few times, but with the help of many little pushes and pulls, Sister Jeremy and thirty-five beaming boys finally reached the playground. I was a new broom, no doubt about that.

The playground extended about a block to a private road, which ran parallel with the west end of the grounds. In spite of the expanse, I felt hemmed in. I could scarcely move backward or forward without stepping on one of the thirty-five. From a respectful distance the older boys were getting the lay of the land, collecting data for future use.

The air was filled with a chorus of mixed voices: "Sister Jeremy, come to see our gardens." "What do you mean, our gardens? They're the big guys' gardens." "Well, my brother has one and I help him pull the weeds." "Yeh, and I help Joey; he's my friend." "Aw, no, come on and see the pets." "They're better; ya kin play with them." "Let's stand by the bridge and watch the goldfish." "How about the diamond, Sister?" "Naw, the dump first." "Aw, gee if ya go to the dump first, ya never get back."

Gardens, dump, pets, diamond, fish, bridge! I was near a bridge already; cross it I must, but I stood there praying silently, "All the days of my life." I must think fast, decide and act quickly.

With a sweeping gesture for silence, I called for a hand-raising vote of those who wanted to go to the gardens first. Majority ruled. We moved slowly—by this time there were about forty. The real gardeners, becoming aware of our intentions, had swelled our number.

Across the private road was the laundry and boilerhouse, to the north of which the boys had their gardens. "Sister Jeremy, my brother has the biggest tomatoes! Come and see," called out Rudy, an aggressive lad who had run ahead of the group.

"Yeh, but look at my peppers," came from Kayo.

"Joey has the biggest head of cabbage."

"It won't be long now, and I will be putting my celery in hills."

Finally Marcellus, a frail lanky fellow, was able to get in what he wanted to tell me. "Sister Jeremy, we ate almost all the lettuce, radishes and onions and some of the other stuff the guys had in their gardens. One day when the things growed big enough, the older boys told Sister Colette they were going to treat us. So Sister Amabilis helped the boys make our meals that day. Gee, Sister, it was good!"

After making the rounds of some thirty plots, I began to wonder how characteristic of the workers these plots were. Some were neatly weeded, vegetables and fruits planted in perfect rows, soil loosened. Others still had unbroken lumps of dirt from early spring when the ground was first turned. Some, lacking plan and arrangement, displayed a variety of weeds and disorder. Time would tell. This was my first evening pinch-hitting for good Sister Colette.

Everyone was still engrossed in gardening when Louie, the tiniest lad in the crowd, yelled, "Sister Jeremy, let's go to the pets now." PETS! Louie's suggestion created a din, somewhat quieted by the sound of curfew for the small boys. Cupping my hands, I called, "Boys, I think you're a great hard-working bunch, but it's time for all young farmers to get ready for bed. Still, I'm puzzled. Why are there only thirty plots, when there are forty-eight big boys and thirty-five smaller ones? Another thing I'd like to know is, why you are so interested in the gardens? Perhaps someone will tell me as we walk back to the building."

"Rudy, you tell Sister Jeremy about the Kiwanis," called Kayo, as the older boys returned to their sports.

"O.K.," agreed Rudy. Marcellus fell in beside Rudy to pick up the seeds of the story which Rudy might happen to let fall. "You see, Sister Jeremy, there are only thirty plots, because not all the kids wanted to have a garden. Some of the guys have other things to do. Anyway, Sister, the Kiwanis Club gave us all the seeds."

73

"Yeh, but Daddy Shoemaker gave the guys seeds, too," piped in Marcellus.

Rudy went on, "The Kiwanis promised to give prizes to the kids that didn't let no weeds grow in their gardens and to the kids that raised the best vegetables and fruits. They're gonna give five prizes. When we're all in school, they come and look at the gardens and mark the prizes."

"Yes, Sister," explained Marcellus with grave assurance; "they write 'first prize' 'second prize' and like that on a stick and put it in the plot that wins."

"That's right, Sister Jeremy, and when they're finished they go to the office and tell Sister Liguori. Then she calls the boys in."

"When the other kids get out of school, they kin all go and see the prize gardens. The Kiwanis tell all the guys why they got a prize and why they didn't get one, so the next time they know what to do."

Back in the building there was a skirmish for towels and places at the foot bath. Another scene was added to Act One. Only momentarily I wondered what part I was to play. My attention was quickly diverted from the foot bath to the calls of "Sister, Sister Jeremy, Sister, you're wanted in the hall."

Stepping into the hall, I was greeted with a pleasant "Good evening, Sister Jeremy, welcome to the Home." It was Sister Bernadette, the bookkeeper. Although I had passed through her office on my arrival at the Home earlier, I had not noticed her. Was she just being cordial, or had I neglected to sign in? Quickly she relieved my questioning mind. "Sister Amabilis can't leave the office. She'd like to see you as soon as you have tucked your charges into bed."

"All right, Sister." I went back to the boys. In a short half hour, thirty-five small fry, washed, pajama-clad, played out and prayed in, lay snug on their pillows. It was nine o'clock. Hoping I had not delayed too long in answering Sister Amabilis' summons, I was on my way to the office framing hundreds of explanations, for what, I did not know. I would walk very quietly and glance into the office before entering. This plan, however, was frustrated by Sister Amabilis' alertness. She noticed me and waved me to her.

Then I saw she had been talking to a thin, tired-looking man. Huddled close to him were three boys about four, seven and nine years old. Their features were definitely Slav. They could have been a Wenceslaus, Ladislas and Casimir, all cut from the same pattern, differing only in size. The waxy whiteness of their skin was accentuated by the cleanliness of their threadbare clothing. The boys looked as though they had come to their execution. As I ruffled the smallest one's curls and admired the love birds he was guarding so carefully, all three looked at me with hungering eyes ranging from blue to deep violet. The man must have read my thoughts as I fixed my gaze on the littlest one. "Eyes like his mother, Sister."

"Sister Jeremy," Sister Amabilis said with a smile to the boys. "These little men have come to live with us. This is their father, Mr. Buda."

The father's callused hand trembled as he pressed mine. "Sister," he confided, "my wife die a month ago. We have the five children. I try to keep them together, but I can't. The baby I give to Mrs. Wilczak, my good neighbor. The oldest, he stay with my sister." He turned to Sister Amabilis. "Is Sister sure she have the room for these three?"

"Of course, Mr. Buda."

He looked down at his boys, his face radiating paternal affection. His eyes dimmed as he added, "I have the hundred dollar left in the bank. In the morning I go to the hospital. If I die, Sister will still take care of my boys, even when the money is used up?"

Sister Amabilis assured him. "This is St. Michael's Home; your boys are ours, Mr. Buda. We'll pray for you—all the Sisters and children."

The parting of father and sons was brief but heartbreaking. This was something I had not been prepared for. With a strange new feeling in my heart I quickly "swallowed" a tear. A new chapter was starting in the lives of three little boys. I wished I could be on hand to watch them grow. Perhaps I might be stationed at St. Michael's and help raise Charlie, four, John, seven, and Joe, nine! Sister Amabilis interrupted my reverie, saying, "Sister Jeremy, I have a few matters to settle before retiring, so I entrust these boys to you." She came over and bent down to them. "Good night, boys! Charlie, Sister Jeremy will take care of your love birds for the night. And you, John, you're going to like it here with us, aren't you?"

John managed a faint smile.

"We'll be real good, Sister," spoke up Joe. "You won't have no trouble with us."

"I know we won't." Sister Amabilis smiled. "Now you trot along with Sister Jeremy."

Night lights were already on when I led the trio to their land of nod. They were very quiet and did not awaken the sleeping portion of the flock. Thanks to the sleep of the innocents only a few heard the soft tiptoeing of the newcomers.

"Dear God, please let these weary lads fall fast asleep without realizing they are away from all that childhood holds most dear," I prayed. Quietly I checked windows, doors, running water and lights in those parts of the building assigned to me. I decided to keep the love birds in my room till next day when they would be added to the accumulation of pets. It was getting late but I must see if Charlie, John and Joe had fallen asleep. They had. "Thanks be to God," I prayed again, "and so to bed."

But it was not to be. Scarcely had I closed my door when I heard a gentle knock. There stood Louie whispering, "Sister, someone is sleeping in the beds where none of the kids should sleep."

Quickly I told him of the three new arrivals and sent him back to sleep. At least, so I thought. But before I had time to close an eye Louie was back with, "Sister Jeremy, Willie is afraid in the dark." Would that it were Louie who was afraid!

Willie was a timid lad of seven who had come in a week ago. He was terribly homesick. His mother was ill, and his father felt that Willie was better off with us.

"Close your eyes, Willie, and you won't see the dark," I said quietly giving him a reassuring pat on the head. After smoothing his coverlet again, I thought the last scene of Act One was finally ended. How little I knew! At once my other charges sat up and began to complain of toothaches, headaches, sore toes and skinned shins.

What they really lacked was love. I felt as if some unknown door in my heart had suddenly swung open, freeing waves of tenderness I had never suspected. Ministering to these hastened the hour of midnight, yet I did rise at five for our prescribed meditation and divine office before Holy Mass.

Those children who wanted to go to Holy Mass arose earlier. The others assembled later in the chapel to offer studies, work and play to the Lord and to ask His blessings on their dear ones and themselves. The Home had one requirement for those who did not rise for Mass; they must remain in bed in silence.

But rules or no rules, Louie had to learn the names of his new companions. Approaching the bedroom door after Mass, I heard whispering. "Ya jist came last night, din'cha? Whatchurname? Who are them other two kids?"

Secrets were not for Louie. In passing to the washroom he blurted, "Sister Jeremy, them kids' names are Charlie, John and Joe, and they got some birds somewhere."

At the same time from the corner sink, I heard, "Hey, kid, whatchurname? Mine's Marcellus."

Marcellus managed to be first in the playroom after breakfast that morning. He brought in the three Budas. "Hey, you guys, this is Charlie. The big guy's Joe and the other one's John. They came while we were in bed. Gee, kid, where'd ja get them swell birds? Whatcha call 'em?"

Charlie smiled timidly. " 'Uv buds."

The boys crowded around Charlie, John and Joe, as the trio guarded their birds carefully. The peacock in the other boys perked up at once. From lockers all kinds of prized possessions tumbled out: pet frogs, model airplanes, marbles, puzzles, movie star pictures and even seeds for next year's watermelon patch. Some of these became the treasures of their new pals.

For a few days I tried to keep a special lookout for the newcomers. They were fighting nobly against homesickness. A few times I found Charlie crying; all three pushed back many a tear. From life in a cozy little bungalow to institutional living was a big jump, even for a brave fellow. Little did they realize that their stay would be a long one. We did not tell them their father's condition was critical. The aunt with whom the oldest boy was living kept this information to herself. Mr. Buda had spent himself to save his wife.

After a brief play period I signaled the children of the lower grades to change from their rough-and-tumbles into school clothes for a short session in the classroom. Sister Amabilis had called the older brood. When I passed her she said, "Sister Jeremy, after your little charges are settled in the classroom, I wish you would supervise a group of the older boys out on the farm."

I recalled hearing or reading somewhere, "He who does not work shall not eat." Since I enjoyed three meals a day, my response was spontaneous. "What is your pleasure, Sister Amabilis?"

"Beans, corn and tomatoes are in demand today for us, and lettuce for the convent. I myself would go to the cornfield with the boys, but if anything comes up in the office, I would be too far from the building. Besides, the lawn needs cutting. From the office I can keep an eye on the boys whose plots of grass are in the front."

She motioned to a group of older boys coming from the diamond. "Jerry, Tony, Carl, Kayo and Whitey, get the lawn equipment to the front yard. I'll be in the office. Report to me as soon as you have all your tools."

"Yes, Sister Amabilis." And the six were off like a flash.

She turned to the other boys waiting for her at the back door. "Pete, you take the key. Mike, Bill and Don, go with Pete to get out the baskets and bags. Leave them in front of the shed; lock the door again and give the key to Sister Jeremy. Wait for Sister and her crew; they'll meet you in the tomato patch. All right, Sister Jeremy. Happy pickin'!" Sister Amabilis went inside.

"Come on, Sister Jeremy, let's go." "Wait, I want a drink first."

Candidly I was not too anxious to be charred. Oh well, what's a little heat to a Franciscan? Quickly I organized my pickers, noting on a piece of paper who was who, for I hadn't yet associated all the older boys' names and faces.

"Why in the world are you tying wet rags around your heads?" I inquired, as we started toward the shed.

The boys all laughed at my puzzlement. "That's so we won't get

78

headaches out in the sun," shouted Bill, who never missed a cue.

"But you'll wear your straw hats . . ."

"Yes, Sister, but we put the wet cloths on too!"

The ingenuity of youth! We were soon trooping down the garden path with "Whistle While You Work" ringing through the air, and baskets and gunny sacks on our arms.

The corn group quickly busied itself filling the gunny sacks. Now and then a call reached my ears: "Sister Jeremy, can you see where I am?" "Sister, can you tell where my row is?" "Yoo hoo, Sister, how far am I?" "Sister, you can't see me," I counted the voices and was almost sure one voice had not called out. Was one of the crew reneging? I would see. The air was carrying "The Sun Shines Bright on My Old Kentucky Home" from the bean pickers' section.

Scarcely had I reached the rows of corn when there was a grand skirmish. Feathers were flying, and blurred figures darted among the stalks. I heard shouts of "Head her off! Over there, Don! Ketch 'er!" It was the missing voice. Darting toward me was a brood of pheasants followed by a disgusted-looking Bill, breathing hard. "The dumb cluck! I wouldn't hurt her for the world."

"Where's your picking, Bill?" I demanded, glaring at his empty sack.

"Gee, Sister, I was seeing how many gopher holes I could count. Then I spied old gopher himself, and if them saps weren't yapping so loud, the little guy would've come out and I'd a' had 'im. Then along comes that dumb cluck and makes little gopher think the whole world is out after him."

"Bill, you realize there's no baseball game this evening for the custodian of any unfinished job, don't you?"

"Custodian? Gee, what's that?" But without waiting for an answer, Bill turned and dashed back to the cornfield. "I'll make it up, 'ster!"

I headed toward the bean patch. Let me see—one little, two little, three little—— I was sure I knew how to count. Try again. One little, two little—nine little bean pickers were all I could see. There were ten on the list pinned to my sleeve. By now I had memorized most of these. Mike? Now which one was Mike? Oh, yes, now I recalled. That blond! But Mike was nowhere to be seen. "Michael, where are you?" There was a chorus of snickers as I scanned the rows. At one end of the patch assigned to Mike there was a slight stir. Was this a case of sunstroke? I hurried to the spot.

There sprawled Mike under the scorching rays of the sun with his hat over his face. I shook him. No response. "Sister, he's dopey; he's always sleeping," said Don, who had followed to watch the fun. I shook him again and Don kicked the sole of his shoe.

"Don," a sleepy voice drawled from under the hat, "get out of here."

"Come on, get to work!" Don urged, with another nudge from his foot.

"Aw, gee, let me alone. Gee, a guy can't even take a sleep." He pulled the hat from his face and sprang up. "Oh, Sister Jeremy, I . . ."

"Yes, Mike," I consoled. "I know Sleeping Beauty never had to pick beans."

Could the tomato patch offer anything more diverting than gophers, pheasants and siestas? When I arrived at the patch two boys were adding another bushel to the baskets and baskets of nice rosy tomatoes already at the head of the rows. "Good for you, Joey and Dave!"

"We're almost finished," said Joey, "but Paul and Bob are 'way behind."

"Oh? But remember," I defended, "Paul and Bob picked a basket of lettuce before they began the tomatoes. Maybe they haven't been junior farmers as long as you."

But Dave quickly informed me, "Oh, yes, they have, Sister. They've both been at the Home longer than Joey and me. Besides, we helped them till they caught up to us."

"Well, that was kind of you."

The two laggards picked faster as I headed toward them. Apart from sheepish glances, everything seemed O.K.

"Paul and Bob, try to get your quota in while we collect the filled baskets for the pick-up truck," I encouraged.

"Yes, 'ster Jeremy," was their strained response, as they gathered tomatoes, not cocking an eye.

Without apologies, "O, My Darling Clementine," was parodied as the pickers pulled along their sacks of corn singing, "O My Darling Little Gopher." Then everyone chanted: "Where do you worka, Mike? I peeck, I peeck, I peeck. What do you peecka, Mike? Da beans, da beans, da beans."

The chant continued: "Take me out to the tomato patch, That's where the field mice you can always catch."

Field mice? Aha! Maybe that was what Paul and Bob . . . I called to the boys. "Assemble at the shed. I'll be with you as soon as I check the tomatoes."

"We're coming, we're coming, for our tomatoes are all picked. We hear you calling, Dave, Paul, Bob and Joe."

"Hail, Hail, the gang's all here!" sang the crew as the last group reached the shed. Bill glanced at me and blurted out, "Sister Jeremy, now that the *custodians* are all *assembled*, kin we go?" Then enjoying the others' baffled looks, he leaned over toward me. "I want to use big words, too, Sister."

I laughed. "Well, Bill, you'll learn!" (As I had in these hours on the farm!) Turning to the tired boys, I announced, "Now you may start in to get cleaned up. You've had your share of sun and heat. I wouldn't run if I were you." We trudged slowly toward the building and I saw Paul and Bob lagging behind. I listened to what was evidently an argument.

"I did not!"

"You did too!"

What were they scrambling for now? Crickets? Grasshoppers?

Bob shouted, "It's all your fault, Mike, you sleepyhead."

"It is not!" snapped Mike, a few paces ahead. "I couldn't help it if the guys shoved me against you. Besides, Sister Amabilis wouldn't let you bring them into the house anyway."

Paul's lettuce leaves dropped to the ground as he whined, "They're gone. I thought I was going to have some trained field mice."

Personal characteristics make no difference at St. Michael's. Jerry, the Jewish boy, shared his pet rabbits with Tony, the Mexican; Whitey, the colored boy, called to Carl, who spoke only Spanish, "Come out with me, Carl, to feed my pretty fantails."

We were walking in the yard after dinner the next day. "Oh,

Sister Jeremy," exclaimed Willie, our seven-year-old Protestant lad, "you never did see our pets, our dump, and all that stuff."

These youngsters constantly tugged at one's heartstrings. I had to be on the alert lest mine become so taut that they would no longer work in accord with my head. To be fair to all, to love each, to give each that for which he was starving—that was our goal. At the same time I had to close my eyes to thoughtlessness, to guide and direct and yet make the boys each realize someone cared.

"Sister Jeremy, ya comin'?" Marcellus took up where Willie left off. "Sister, pleeeeeeese! You're here so long, and you didn't go with us to our old dump yet."

"Well, I'll make a bargain with you." I stopped, and they crowded around me.

"What's a bargain, 'Ster? Is it like when we swap?" All the chatter died away.

"Yes, something like that. Are you ready for the bargain?"

"Yes, 'Ster, yes 'Ster, yes 'Ster!" came from all sides.

"You say, 'Yes, Sister,' but you might change your mind when you hear what I ask," I teased.

"No, we won't! Honest!" they insisted.

"Well, here's my plan. It's time for class now. Later during your story hour, we'll take a walk to the dump. Then, instead of my telling *you* a story, you tell me one—all about the dump."

"Hooray!" they shouted.

That afternoon at two o'clock we set out on our tour. Whitey began, "Sister, all this place along the road is what we call our dump. Long time ago people used to throw all kinds of junk here. We cleared it all out. Pulled the weeds, cut the grass and raked until it looked nice like this."

"Seester Cheremee, first come here!" pleaded Carl, gesticulating vigorously. He was standing before a rock formation which encircled a tall white statue of Our Lady of Lourdes.

"But the boys didn't make that," I exclaimed.

"Oh, yes, they did!" Whitey and Carl nodded emphatically.

"That tree was dead, so the guys scooped out holes and filled 'em with dirt and planted them ivies. The vine and them flowers over there we got from a man who owns a flower joint. He saw us working and asked if we wanted some help. Next day he brought us all these plants. We wrote him a letter and thanked him, too."

Jerry was tugging at my sleeve. "The zoo, Sister Jeremy!"

"The zoo, the zoo, the zoo!" They all chimed in and steered me beyond the shrine to a little fenced-in enclosure at the bottom of the hill. With Jerry at my side I heard all about his baby alligator, the pet turtle, the doves and the bunnies.

"An' here's the pond, Sister," directed Tony a little farther down. "My brudder Joe and Rudy's cousin used to be here. They're out workin' now, but they come ta see us sometimes. When they saw the big guys that work in the print shop makin' the pond, the win'-mill, and the bridge fer us when they didn't have ta work in the shop, Joe and Rudy's cousin said they would buy us the goldfish fer the pond. Whenever they see a different kind of fish they buy it fer us."

"Do you know how many you have?" I asked.

"Oh, yes, 'Ster," came a chorus of voices. "You can't fool us! We count 'em every day." Now I knew why I often saw the little fellows lying flat on their tummies near the pond.

"Boys, this has been a very interesting story," I said as we started back. Just then Rudy planted himself in front of me, one hand over the other like a prima donna at an opera. "Well, Rudy, do I get a solo now?" Not knowing what I meant, he uncupped his hands. Two or three little fuzzy yellow creatures moved over his fingers. "Rudy, those bees will sting you," I warned. But Rudy knew his pets and only laughed.

That night when the children were all in bed I was drinking in the quiet of summer from the north corridor window. The lights of the heavy highway traffic blinked and flashed like myriads of fireflies, and made fairylike patterns that held me fascinated. A jingle of rosary beads sounded faintly in the dark, and Sister Amabilis stood beside me. Somehow I knew she was smiling.

"You've been doing beautifully, Sister Jeremy."

"Thanks, Sister. With God's help I hope I'll finish the week without any major disaster."

"That's what I'd like to talk to you about. Oh, not a major disaster, but a minor eruption here and there is often likely."

"Well, come on, Sister, let's sit down on the settee by the night light," I invited.

"Oh, it won't take long. You see, Sister, some of the children have come to the Home very recently. When the novelty of their new abode wears off, they may become very shy or strange or bold with homesickness. Sensitiveness makes their tempers flare, and things happen that would not normally be expected."

"Like what, please?" I asked, knowing only the familiar classroom mischiefs.

"Well," Sister replied, "one or the other might decide that we are not able to cope with his affairs, that we don't understand him. He might hide a bundle in some dark corner and, when the house is quiet some night, sneak out and make for the highway."

The task of caring for others' children loomed before me as a tremendous responsibility.

"Sister Amabilis," I gasped, "do I stay up all night and make rounds counting heads? If I discover one missing, what do I do? Make for the highway myself?" I was getting panicky. "Do I sound the siren? Tell me, what should I do?"

"You just stay calm. A housemother is a composite of Fairy Godmother, Good Samaritan and Guardian Angel. And none of these characters has ever been known to panic. Don't worry—boys have run away before. We merely phone the police. Never has anyone gone farther than Tannerton or Paddock. Often they turn back before the police even find them." She laughed and told me the following incident.

One late afternoon a few years previously, three of the younger senior boys took to the road. Cleverly evading the police, they got as far as the convent in Tannerton, when darkness robbed them of their bravery. They huddled together in a doorway under a high porch, trying in excited whispers to decide what to do next. It started to rain. They were hungry and chilly. By chance that night, Mother Regina herself was going down that way. Her keen ears

detected whispers, and she opened the door to confront the cul-
prits. "Who are you?" she asked, towering above them.

Shakily one of them replied, "We . . . we're from St. Michael's
Home."

"St. Michael's Home?" echoed Mother. "But this isn't St. Michael's Home."

"We—uh—we lost our way. W-would you please call Sister
Liguori an'—an' tell her we're here?"

"I don't understand. Where did you expect Sister Liguori to be?"
But no answer this time. Their heads hung. "Oh, I see." Mother
smiled secretly. "You want me to call Sister and tell her that the
boys who ran away want to come back. Is that it?"

The heads came up with a sigh of relief. "Yes, Sister."

"You had better come inside now. What are your names?"
Mother Regina brought them into the hall.

The only one who had spoken thus far identified himself as
Mike. "An' that's Don an' Kayo."

"Well, just sit down here while I call the Home. Sister Liguori
will be glad you're here, I'm sure." In a moment she returned. "Don,
why didn't you go to the corner store and phone Sister Liguori
yourself?"

"We were afraid they would call the police."

Kayo added, "We thought 'cuz you're the same 'Sters ez take
care of us at St. Michael's you'd listen to us."

"We're sorry we ran away," said Kayo, looking at his shoes.

The episode ended in a happy reunion.

"It's very rare," Sister Amabilis continued, "That a runaway is
brought back without deep contrition. We housemothers have
learned to put our trust in God completely. After all, aren't we all
His children—prodigal and otherwise?"

Pondering this morsel of wisdom, I went to bed and slept as
soundly as any of my young charges. In my dreams I saw the smiling
face of Sister Olivia.

Next morning Sister Amabilis met me in the playroom. "Sister
Jeremy, the mending is piling up. After the boys are in the class-

room, we'd better check their clothes. What doesn't need mending we can put away, so the job won't seem so enormous."

"Mending?" I gaped at the multicolored mountain of clothes on the table.

The mending for our harum-scarum lads was a veritable Matterhorn. Sister Amabilis had already put her deft hands to the task. "Sister Jeremy, recall our Latin proverb, '*Labor omnia vincit*.' We'll level this by pure, unadulterated labor." She was already fitting a patch into a knee hole. "And while I think of it, Sister, our little lambs are getting woolly. We'd better keep a few of them in the playroom this afternoon and shear their golden fleece."

"What's this?" I asked incredulously.

"Sister Jeremy, how do you think a boy keeps his male look? Do you think we singe his hair?"

I had never given hair cutting a thought. But now it dawned on me; if only one boy got a hair cut each week, by the time the last would have his, on the thirty-eighth week, the first one would look like a young Samson.

At noontime, before dismissing the boys for outdoors, I announced, "St. Michael's barbershop will open at one o'clock. The names of the first six customers will be put on the bulletin board."

The third lamb was being shorn, when a pleasant, jovial man's voice came from the doorway: "Say, Sisters, you can't do that! You're taking wages from a good honest union barber!"

"Oh, Uncle Charlie!" Sister Amabilis cried joyfully. "Come in. Sister Jeremy, this is my Uncle Charlie, an old faithful of the Home. What brings you here at this hour of the day?"

"You haven't forgotten barbers work only half a day on Wednesday, have you? I told the family I'd drive to the country for fresh eggs. Your big welcome sign in the front yard tempted me. Come on, give me that apron. I'll show you how a barber does the trick." And he was soon snipping away expertly. Marcellus was delighted at the change of hands.

"Why, Uncle Charlie, you haven't a very good opinion of our tonsorial ability, have you?" laughed Sister Amabilis.

"A little slow, I would say. Is this the last one?"

"Oh, no, this is only the first batch."

"Listen, Sister, I've got to be on my way now. Can't keep the family waiting. But I'll be back later. O.K. with you? Judging from facial expressions, it's tops with Sister Jeremy."

True to his word, Uncle Charlie returned even earlier than we expected, well equipped with barber's accessories. Little Willie was the first on his list. After his haircut he went back to play. Louie kept following him around, and one of the boys heard Louie say, "Mmm, Willie, you smell so nice." The older boys were right outside the window settling the lineup for the next day's ballgame. Jerry dashed over to the window calling: "Hey, you big guys, I got a real haircut. Louie says it smells nice."

Bill, who was always precise about his personal appearance, came near to look Jerry over. "Quite snazzy, I would say, Jerry. Were you to town today?"

"Naw, I jist got it here in the playroom. A real barber is here."

"Gee, kids, do you think he's gonna cut our hair too?" came from Kayo.

"Couldn't say, Kayo, couldn't say. Why doncha ask him?" And Jerry ran off to play.

Inside, Uncle Charlie was still snipping away. "Sister Amabilis, why didn't I think of this before?"

"Think of what?"

"Oh, never mind, I guess a flash bulb just burned out. Would it be O.K. with you if I quit after this one? I'd like to see a few of the older boys. I'll do more hair next week. Sister Jeremy, after your good patrolling job for my customers, would you like to take over? I'm quitting for now."

"Uncle Charlie, you don't know what a great big favor you've done today. Thank you, and God bless you over and over again."

Sister Amabilis gathered the older boys for Uncle Charlie just outside the back door. "Any of you fellows who aren't interested in wire don't have to stay, if it's O.K. with Sister." Everyone wanted to stay. That settled, Sister Amabilis supervised the young tykes and completed urgent office matters, giving me the opportunity to stay with Uncle Charlie's group. Pointing them out with a slap on the back, Uncle Charlie said, "You and you and you come with me to the car. The rest wait. We'll be back in a jiffy."

At the car the boys pulled out a large roll of wire and several pairs of big wire snippers. Back with the group, Uncle Charlie stood in full view, measured a length of wire, cut it off and began twisting. "You see," he said, "a barber cuts so much wire in a week that it's a shame to throw it away, so he tries to find some particular use for it."

They laughed uproarously. "Aw, you're jist kiddin' us now," drawled Kayo.

"Kidding you? Why would I want to kid you?" Soon as he held up the wire thing in its crude shape, there was a volley of shouts, "Oh, boy!" "Yippee!" "Wahoo!" "Whoopie!" "Just what we need for our wienie roasts!" "A wienie fork!" "A wienie fork!" Exclamations petered out, with each busily fashioning a wire, and Uncle Charlie saying, "Now we'll have to try these out. Sister, if you'll have several scouts build a fire in the fireplace, I'll drive a couple of the boys to the All Hour Market and get a few pounds of wieners."

Early Thursday morning honor points were checked. An announcement was then to be made as to who was eligible for the hike that day. Just as Sister Amabilis was about to tell the exciting news, her signal rang. In the interim the boys sought me out with a barrage of questions. "Sister, am I going on the hike?" and "Are you coming with us?" were the leads.

Shortly Sister Amabilis returned, telling me, as I went to meet her, "Sister Jeremy, Uncle Charlie's flash bulb went on again. Last evening he contacted the president of the Barber's Association and some of the members. The results are: quote—The first Tuesday of each month ten to fifteen volunteer barbers will have the honor of cutting all the children's hair—end of quote. Won't Sister Ligouri be happy when she hears the news!"

"Oh, that's grand! God bless their hearts and hands!" I rejoined.

"Come to think of it, Sister Jeremy," she continued as we approached the boys, "you do like to walk? Would you care to hike with the boys today? I'll be happy to oversee the younger ones while you're gone."

"That would be great. Thank you, Sister."

"Come on, Sister Amabilis, we can't wait!" called Pete as he spied us coming.

"Boys, the honor points show that all but two of you may go for a hike. Sister Jeremy will go with you. Joey can't go because of his fractured ankle. But don't worry, Joey." She turned to him. "You may ride out in the car with the lunch."

"Yippee!" squealed Joey.

"You may hike to the DuPage River just beyond Daniels' farm."

"DuPage! DuPage!" yelled the entire crowd.

The half dozen smaller boys who would be eligible to join the older group in September had been given permission to go along. This was not favorably received by the older boys, who feared their progress would be hindered. Last minute chores were completed, good-bys, cheers and songs rent the air, as the group started off on the seven-mile trek in the sweltering heat on an August day in Tannerton.

"Why do you young runts want to come along anyway?" growled Paul as the younger ones slowed up.

"We wanna have some fun, too," answered the ever alert Marcellus.

"If you holler at him again," chimed in Rudy, "I'll get my bees after you."

Tweet, tweet, tweet!

The hilarious hikers hardly realized how far ahead they had strayed when Don yelled: "Stop! *Halt!* You mugs up ahead, didn'ja hear Sister Jeremy's whistle?"

After a glance back, one after the other began to fling himself in the grass by the roadside. Their chatter ceased as I called: "Boys, let's make this a hike, not a race. Please keep together. Now you may continue."

"O.K. 'Ster."

"Sister Jeremy, maybe it would help if we put them young kids between the older guys," Bob suggested. "Don and I will take care of them."

I agreed. "That's what I call Christian kindness—real love for one's fellow men."

Three miles must have been covered when Bob noticed that Jerry had stopped. "What's the matter?" called Bob.

"Nothin'—just keep goin'! I'll ketch up with ya." He did—with his shoes under his arm instead of on his feet.

"Jerry, who do you suppose is going to mend those socks?" I queried as I looked at his stockinged feet.

"Really, Sister," piped in Don, "do you think he'll have any socks left when we get home?"

Most of us were wilted by the hot sun when we heard the leaders' call, "DuPage ahead! Just a little farther now."

"Here we are, Sister Jeremy!" Lightning-like, they zoomed toward the cool riverbank. After such a hike, I expected everyone to sit quietly for a while and rest. "You younger ones," I urged, "better stay here in the shade until you cool off a bit."

"Then kin we go fishin'?" asked Rudy.

After a short jaunt in the woods Bill and Kayo announced their return with, "Here, Sister Jeremy, we made fishin' poles for the young punks."

"That's the way to have a lot of fun! Try to help others have fun, too."

Honk, honk! All heads turned toward the incoming car.

Whichever way I looked, the hikers were heading for reinforcements with cries of, "Sister Jeremy, look who's coming! Oooooooh, goooody, I'm starved." "Me, too." "Steve! Three cheers for Steve, Gene and the eats." "Boy, oh, boy, when do we eat?"

Joey hobbled over to me saying, "Sister Jeremy, meet Steve and Gene—they used to be at the Home. They're working now. They brought the lunch for the guys."

I looked up at two young men of about nineteen. "Glad to make your acquaintance, Sister Jeremy. How do you like taking care of a gang like this along the river?"

"It's quite a job all right, but thank God, everyone's Guardian Angel has been doing a marvelous job."

Turning to the gang, Steve said, "You kids go sit along the riverbank till Sister blows her whistle. Oh, pardon me, Sister, I didn't mean to boss. I only wanted to be a little helpful. You see we can't stay long. We explained to the foreman where we were going but we don't want to delay too long."

A few of the fellows carried the food from the car while Gene built the fire for the wieners and marshmallows. Proudly the boys used their hand-made wiener forks as each took care of a younger pal who had none. What opportunities, I thought, were given these youngsters to develop the art of living happily and harmoniously with others! As soon as "Operation Food" was well under way, Steve and Gene came over to me again. "Well, Sister Jeremy, hope you have a good time. Gene and I'll be heading back to town. Come on, Joey, we can't leave you here." On the way to the car Steve called back, "Any of you guys want a ride home? Come along!" No one budged.

That evening Steve, Gene and three other former boys drove to the Home. Not finding the hikers, Steve left the four and went to meet the tired, happy group. The luggage and the younger boys were crowded into his car. The others shouted, "Good-by, don't come back for us. We want to finish the hike."

Paul waved them off, sighing contentedly, "Gee, now we kin git somewhere. No more luggage, no more slowpokes."

When we finally arrived home, Joey met us at the outer door. "Shh! Shh! Quiet, please."

"Why the hush, Joey? What gives?" asked Don.

As we tried to enter the playroom guards greeted us with solemn faces and downcast eyes.

"Sister Jeremy," whispered Joey, "would you care to view the corpse? Sister Amabilis has taken the chief mourner to bed. Funeral services will be held tomorrow morning before school starts."

Tiptoeing to a small table draped in mourning, I found a small feathery body lying in a velvet-lined cigar box with dandelions and sweet clover blossoms spread in various shapes around it. Evidently the stay-at-homes had had sufficient handicraft to keep them out of mischief.

The next morning the funeral procession made its way to the cemetery, where other pets had been buried under the weeping willow tree. So downcast was the chief mourner that he was unaware of the cortege of more than a hundred children. Already in place was a beautiful marker which the boys had fashioned by cementing together some of their most colorful marbles. And they laid to rest one of our dear Charlie's love birds.

"Extra! Extra! Extra! Just off the press! Latest edition of *St. Michael's Messenger!*" echoed through the halls as Pete, the junior apprentice, brought the *Messenger* to the housemothers.

The St. Michael's printers were older orphan boys who made St. Michael's their home even after graduation because of their regard for their profession. The oldest printer was also captain of our baseball team. However, he would sacrifice his favorite sport to be on deck for a job. The wide-eyed younger boys often voiced their aspirations with "I'm going to be a printer when I get with the big boys."

Besides the *Messenger*, the boys also did printing for schools and parishes of the community as well as for various business places. Most of the copy was hand-set, although occasionally a commercial establishment would linotype the matter, turning it over to the boys for completion.

As a novice I had been initiated into typesetting as well as the rudiments of the press. Then printing was in experimental stages at the convent. And so I could appreciate the boys' work. Maybe I would be assigned to St. Michael's this year. If so I would be glad for my brief experience. I could still be a printer's devil; could make pi; could measure by ems and ens instead of by centimeters and millimeters; above all, I had not forgotten to mind my P's and Q's.

I perused my *Messenger* with interest. The summer activities, the change in personnel, the list of benefactors—all were duly reported in refreshing, youthful style.

From where I stood reading I could hear Bill yell: "Hey, you

92

guys, take a slant at the bulletin board. Sister Amabilis sure has an eye for business!"

"What's up now?" "What's the gag?" queried one, then another. "Yeh! Yeh!" thundered through the building. Attracted by claps and yells, the younger boys came running to see what was happening. The older ones were methodically hurrying here and there, heeding none of the curious questions put to them. Rudy hopped on a chair and read aloud:

NOTICE

1. The grass has not all been cut this week.
2. The ruts in the driveway are very hard on cars.
3. More than flowers are growing in the plots around the shrine.
4. When was the hedge last trimmed?

SPECIAL—The captain of the Clover Farm Team called this morning to schedule a game for this afternoon. I told him our captain would give him the answer by noon.

BOYS—The answer depends on the above four points.

SR. M. A.

Jumping down, Rudy explained: "Kids, that means if the big guys git their work done this morning, we'll have a baseball game today."

Shouts went up again, and the crowd scattered, excitedly speculating. They knew the chores would be done in record time.

"Sister Jeremy, you'll let your kids watch the game today, won't you?" pleaded Captain Joe, as we answered the dinner bell. "You see, Sister, your young kids will cheer for us and heckle Clover Farm's pitcher so we can win. They're tough birds to beat."

"But, Joe, you know the younger ones go to school."

"Yes, Sister, but if I ask Sister Amabilis, I think she would let them come down at two o'clock. Then you could see the game too." He caught his breath. "Besides, when Sister Liguori is home and St. Michael's has a game scheduled with the Clover Farm team, Sister Liguori permits the girls' housemother to cancel their regular duties so they can come out and see the game. Sister Jeremy, I guess

93

you don't know how the girls help win games. They have formed a special group who are the cheer leaders. The job they do in practicing and perfecting the cheers for our games is wonderful. When your guys come to the games, the cheer leaders get them in the rooting mood too. Kayo, Pete and Bill have sisters among the cheer leaders. You should see my team play when their girl friends are cheering!"

"Joe, I'd love to swell the ranks of the rooters. Also, I'd like to see St. Michael's Team use their diamond and home plate. You make the deal with Sister Amabilis, and we'll be there thirty-nine strong."

What a game! St. Michael's won in the tenth inning by a score of 5-4, as the rooters yelled, "We won!!! We won!!!"

We were sitting in the yard after the game when Bob spied a familiar car. "Hey, here comes Steve and Gene!"

The two alumni sauntered over to us, grinning and grabbing hands of the small throng that ran to meet them.

"Hi, Sister Jeremy, how do you feel after your hike?" asked Steve.

"Just a wee bit footsore, but it was loads of fun," I replied.

"Where's our chief mourner?" inquired Gene, scanning faces. "Oh, there you are, Charlie! Sister, do you mind if we take Charlie over to the car for a minute?"

With the first real grin since his "bereavement," Charlie came bouncing back holding a little cage with a new love bird in it. "Good-by, gang!" echoed from the car and Steve and Gene drove off.

Sunday was my last day at St. Michael's. About nine o'clock that morning, the Sisters returned from the mother house with appointment news. After my term at St. Albert's, I had every reason to be doubtful about the next year's assignment. Here it comes, I thought, St. Michael's Home. ". . . and in obedience all the days of my life" was revolving in my mind as I met Sister Liguori and the others in the entrance.

"Sister Jeremy." Sister Liguori smiled.

Yes, I thought, it's going to be St. Michael's. Although I would miss St. Albert's, I would love it here. But I found a big smile on my face when I heard the message: "Sister Basil left word you are to travel with the last group tomorrow evening for St. Albert's."

As I packed, I felt a growing urge to share the delightful episodes of my stay at St. Michael's. I looked forward to regaling St. Albert's staff with the boys' antics. But I felt that old lump in my throat as I murmured to myself, "Sister Olivia—if I could only tell you!" When I waved good-by to Charlie and Rudy, Bill and the rest, I felt somehow she did know and was smiling—yes, a little proudly.

Chapter Five

The September breeze fanned my cheek gently. It was good to be back at St. Albert's. As I wandered in the courtyard in the late afternoon one September day, a million things distracted me from the rosary I was trying to pray. Sturdy zinnias in the neighbors' yard daringly flaunted their brilliant yellows, reds and purples. Passing by, a little girl in braids singsonged, "Good afternooooon, Sister!" A robin tugged at a fat worm in the tiny patch of grass near the church wall. A wave of happiness surged through me. This was home for another year—St. Albert's.

Then I wondered—was this what my novice mistress meant by attachment? I wondered what it would be like not to be reassigned to St. Albert's. Mechanically my fingers moved to the next bead of my rosary. The Fourth Mystery! With dismay I corralled my thoughts. I determined to concentrate on the rosary I was praying. I closed my eyes, but I could not shut out the touch of God's breeze and the tangy scent of Ohio's autumn.

My heart lifted in joy again. Every experienced teacher knows the pleasure of giving her very self, her thoughts, ideas, emotions, to well-ordered and receptive classes. In my September fervor, I was sure the boys and girls at St. Albert's were different from all others in a dozen ways; they were a choice bit of humanity placed here in this Ohio promised land. Their respectful frankness was charming, their goodness and enthusiasm endearing.

In such a satisfied frame of mind, I surprised Sister Ida one day in the community room shortly after school opened by declaring, "I think I'll start a science club."

Sister Ida did not even miss a stitch on the altar lace she was crocheting. I watched her, waiting until she counted the stitches to a convenient stop. I had all the answers ready for all her objections.

Sister Ida finished her count, laid her lace with deliberate care in her lap, gazed at me fixedly, and then asserted, more than questioned, "Have you lost your mind?"

Of course it would mean much extra work, I agreed. But so did everything worth while. What if clubs at St. Albert's had been failures before? What if the voluntary service on the part of the students had been lacking? One could at least try. But her final remark took the wind out of my sails, "Besides, I don't think the principal will approve."

There was only one way to find that answer, I argued. Sister Basil was examining with obvious pleasure some chemistry notebooks when I entered her office. Hopefully I prayed that the moment was auspicious.

Even though I had outgrown the "little-girl-penny-purchaser" feeling in her absence, I had only advanced to the adolescent. I still felt incapable and awkward. I was sure she would think the venture beyond my capabilities. Her disconcerting way of scrutinizing me while pondering the advisability of granting a request gradually disappeared. "Sister Mary Jeremy," she declared at last with one of her rare smiles, "I think you have an excellent idea."

In a weak, high-pitched voice I thanked her and hurried from the room.

True to her good nature, Sister Ida was a loyal colleague in planning an undertaking that she had first opposed. To her exceptional organizational ability and foresight, I owed much of the club's success. To limit the membership, we held a written test for all juniors and seniors who wanted to join.

Each aspiring member was also required to write an essay on his hobby or to demonstrate it at a general assembly for the upperclassmen. After we had evaluated the hobbies and the test results, the science faculty recommended twenty-two students as charter members of the club. So many applicants went on the waiting list that the chosen twenty-two were more alert than ever, afraid of jeopardizing their position. The day after their acceptance, while I was in the lab preparing apparatus for the next day's experiment, they wrangled in youthful fashion over the formulation of a constitution, membership rules and a name for the club.

These boys and girls had a variety of traits and talents. Bob—Red's brother—was handsome, slim and sturdy, with an attitude that seemed to defy anyone to teach him anything. Somewhere he had acquired the idea that the classroom was a place to torture teachers by apparent indifference. Yet he had scored third highest in the test and was the best ham radio operator in the city. Bob's brother Jim was also his classmate. A little older and larger in build, Jim was pleasant, less talented than Bob, but ambitious. Jack, blond, happy-go-lucky, always mimicking Mark Twain characters, was popular. He was one of a family of eight boys and a brother of Fred.

Herman, mechanically minded, was not too interested in theory. He could repair anything. Lecture periods would have dragged out interminably for him if he had not always managed to be assembling a gadget while he listened. His fingers looked as though he used them for screw drivers, his hands for hammers and his teeth for monkey wrenches. To prevent his neighbors in class from following his techniques, I asked him to take the last place in the room. Occasionally he would deign to question a theoretical point.

Ray, a small, wiry lad, was the sunshine of the classroom—any teacher's morale builder. Whether or not he always knew what I was talking about, he acted as though he did. Watches were his hobby. For my convenience I seated him in front of the room. He knew how to dissemble and assemble intricate mechanisms and I let him demonstrate now and then. He never caused any trouble except that he sometimes sent a sign-language message across the room to Mary Jo, his life-long girl friend. Mary Jo was the epitome of neatness. Her class assignments were always on time, as perfect as she could make them. She was attentive and exact in the laboratory. Dorothy was the sister of Eugenia of the famous oxygen experiment. Popular with both boys and girls, she was careful and deliberate like Eugenia, but not so meticulous.

"Heck, no, Dorothy," Jack objected, as I fitted the last piece of apparatus into place. "That's girls' stuff!"

"If Parliamentary procedure," Dorothy replied loftily, "is good enough for the Congress of this great nation, it ought to be good enough for St. Albert's Science Club. And it's not girls' stuff, either."

They were on their own. There were no retiring types among them. Finally the constitution took shape. Membership rules and meeting procedures were well outlined. If the club fulfilled its purpose it would make not only these students more scientific-minded, but the entire student body more aware of scientific phenomena. The principal marveled.

At the October meeting they chose the name Marconian Club, honoring Guglielmo Marconi, their contemporary Catholic scientist. The newly elected president, Jack, in his first self-conscious moments of presiding, called it the Macaroni Club.

Jack's first official move was to call for discussion of an agenda for the year. While I listened to their cavalcade of ideas, I became more and more convinced that a club could be a perpetual problem. Suggestions kept prancing by—"Mr. Chairman, Jim. I move that we have a mock radio broadcast." "Let's have an amateur night." "I think it would be nice to make a field trip to Washington research laboratories; my brother is a chemist there." "Why not a field trip through Franklin Park? Or through the water works plant? Or a trip through the dial telephone system?"

Ray asked for the floor. "Mr. Chairman, let's have a science congress. We could exhibit our own models and invite students from other schools to show theirs. We could make it go over big. Maybe have it at Memorial Hall." The group responded lustily, voicing their spirited approval.

At my place in the rear of the room I had been virtually forgotten. No one noticed my dismay. I knew Ray's idea would be accepted. Then my problems would be worse than they were now with the project I had allowed Ray to work out on his own. For weeks I had been sweeping him out of the laboratory after school. Ray had planned to make a glass model steam-heating system for a two-story home. First he had asked me for some glass tubing. Absent-mindedly, I had consented, thinking he wanted a foot or two of it. He had already used up almost the entire year's supply. The glass radiators were perfectly shaped. A flask served as the boiler. The glass traps were all set; only one or two radiators were still missing in his model house. But the laboratory looked like a plumber's shop.

Other problems suggested themselves as their discussion heightened during that first meeting of the Science Club. The laboratories were not adequate for more than two projects at a time. What if ten students decided on similar projects? Besides, how many students would persevere to produce a masterpiece like Ray's? I felt the newborn club should learn to walk before it entered a track race.

As moderator I needed tact. I would have to be subtle in getting Ray's idea of a science congress put aside. I raised my hand and stood. "Mr. Chairman, Sister Jeremy."

"Sister Jeremy" was Jack's serious recognition.

"The science congress is a great idea, but it would take much time and many arrangements, and since we're all new at this business, shouldn't we start with something less complicated?" I noticed gratefully that a few of the conservatives were nodding agreement.

"How about planning some interesting monthly meetings? Why not join the Film Rental Club of Ohio State University? Then we might show movies at several meetings. The program committee could prepare a movie schedule to correlate classroom subject matter. I'm sure the science faculty would submit their course outlines to guide you."

This directed the club to form a specific plan for the November meeting. The special feature was a skit on the life of Marconi and the history of communication. The program committee had received excellent co-operation. Various posters and projects of model telephones from the one-wire type to the combined receiver-and-sender type complemented the skit. At this November meeting Ray asked for the floor and suggested a field trip to the dial telephone system. I instructed Ray, the program committee chairman, to arrange it with the Bell Telephone Company. The secretary was to post the notice on the lab Bulletin Board when time and date were definite.

The November meeting adjourned with all in high spirits and

ready to take over the scientific world. I waited days. No sign of any field trip. The Marconian section of the bulletin board remained blank. To take action or not to take action—that was my question. And what action?

As I hurried through the court one day, deep in thought, I noticed Jack stepping out of the principal's office. Seeing me, he called, "Sister Jeremy, the club's touring the telephone company tomorrow afternoon."

"Good, Jack," I said meekly. "I must have missed the bulletin board announcement."

"Bulletin board, Sister? Why I just now used the principal's phone to call."

I gasped. As if to spare me the embarrassment of a caustic remark, the principal stepped out of her office and asked, "Sister, did you send Jack in here to put in a call?"

The principal, Jack and I weighed the situation. We studied how to tie the loose strings. A mollified Jack apologized to Ray, the club's secretary, and then asked him to post the announcement on the bulletin board.

For the December and January meetings we featured free movies from the Ohio State Film Library. Club members also gave reports and original skits on the lives of the scientists and on scientific matters like the latest developments in synthetics.

One of the planned field trips was to Batelle Memorial Institute in Columbus. The guide who conducted the lecture tour persuaded the students that his institution was really fulfilling its motto, "We Improve Everything." Another high light of the club's first year was the visit to the cyclotron of Ohio State University. In those days atom smashing was still a novelty. Seeing the atom smasher stirred the inventor in the soul of each club member. Subsequently I was deluged with designs for atom smashers. Sometime, somewhere, in a methods class I had been told to recognize all students' work. I pinned their atom smasher designs on the bulletin board and hoped that no visitors would chance by until the designs were removed.

As the Science Club flourished, the curve of classroom interest mounted. But to date, all activities had been the result of my direct guidance. Originally I had wanted the club to function differently. Before the next regular meeting I called a special meeting of the officers. "This is your club," I informed them. "It's time for you to take over. You plan the agenda for the February meeting. I'll let you assume the entire responsibility for the program."

Jack, the chairman, slowly untangled his legs at regulation Ohio speed, and eased up his full six feet four inches. He glanced at me but peered at the group and finally drawled, "O.K., gang, we'll do it." Then he assured me, "Sister, don't worry about a thing. We'll plan the whole meeting."

The officers applauded, and Jack drew himself up another inch. Ceremoniously he lifted a stray strand of blond hair from his eye and put it in place.

I had a few qualms about this Mark Twain fan. After school, while I arranged material for the next day's experiments, Jack usually followed me around the lab, reading choice anecdotes from Mark Twain. "You and Mark Twain be hanged!" I was half-tempted to ejaculate more than once. But I locked my ears to all vibrations, fixed a half smile on my lips and kept on setting up my experiments.

Jack was an inveterate late-comer too. One day Sister Ida determined to lock him out of the senior bungalow the next time he was tardy to compel him to make up the lost time later. Shortly after, on a sunny afternoon, the clock ticked regularly toward twelve-thirty. Sister Ida walked to the back door of the classroom, planning to lock it as soon as the second bell rang. She reached for the knob. But just then Jack poked his head in the door and surprised her with, "Sister, look at all the termites!" Triumphantly he pointed at the swarm of insects at the bungalow base. Sister Ida didn't look, she stared. Jack stepped inside and casually glided to his desk.

Days went by as school days do. The officers of the club showed no signs of extra activity. I was afraid there would be no program, but I determined not to meddle. Two days before the meeting, Jack sauntered up. "Sister, we're going to have a little play for our next meeting."

103

"A play? That's fine." I beamed. "Did you find it in a periodical?"

"Oh, no. We made it up," he explained in an aggrieved tone.

Mark Twain, termites, tardiness and a dozen other notions pinwheeled through my head. "Made it up?" I asked weakly. "Well, that's original! What's the name of it? Are you sure—?"

But Jack was confident. "Oh, everything is O.K., Sister. It's called 'The Lion Tamer.' Don't worry. All you have to do is to be on time for the meeting."

"Lion Tamer!" I stammered to myself. It must be an application of zoölogy. I was on time—five minutes before time, to be exact.

The laboratory wore its usual tumbled-over, three-o'clock look. Preparations for a meeting were nowhere apparent. In fact, no one was in sight.

Two minutes later Jack, with a flourish, escorted the principal into the laboratory, drew a chair into the middle of the room and seated her ceremoniously. A quick glance out of the west window revealed other members recruiting an audience. Homebound freshies were being removed from their bicycles and propelled labward. I groaned an ejaculation to the Saint of the Impossible.

Suddenly two of the shortest members of the club were asked to hold a sheet as the curtain for an imaginary stage at the front of the room. They stretched the sheet perpendicular to the row of glass cases near the west windows. Strutting up from the rear, Jack scanned his audience. He struck the gavel and demanded silence. Then he pompously announced the title of the play, "The Lion Tamer." For about thirty seconds the lower part of him disappeared behind the sheet. When he reappeared, he pinned a large sign on the sheet, LION TAMER WANTED. The procession of applicants ranged from wizened, gopherlike girls to stalwart he-men. They came from everywhere in the audience. As each applied, Jack momentarily removed the sign from the curtain and walked behind it. One by one, the applicants met the same fate. A roaring and a hullaballoo arose behind the curtain and then a cap and jacket came flying over the curtain. Each time, Jack would reappear to pin up the sign, LION TAMER WANTED.

In sheer desperation I was about to intervene when I saw Ray amble up to apply for the job. The roaring behind the sheet became fiercer than ever before. Of a sudden a bone, nine inches long and two or three inches wide, hurtled over the curtain, barely missing the glass case. The principal gasped. Jack came out with Ray and the new sign, LION WANTED. Both bowed. The audience clapped. The show was over.

An elated Jack announced the adjournment of the meeting and proudly escorted the principal back to her office, complacent about what he obviously thought was a program with an original twist. To this day the principal has never mentioned "The Lion Tamer."

The Marconians needed a lion tamer and no bones about it. Their program had exceeded any teacher's professional nightmares. Jack called the officers together at my request for a meeting after school hours on the first available date. I felt like old Cicero as I deluged them with a series of rhetorical questions: "What is your idea of science? Of a science club? Of a science program? Of a science meeting? What preparation ought to be made for a meeting? What happened to the original constitution that you labored over so conscientiously? What about your original agenda? Did you have a business meeting of the board before the program? What does the word moderator mean? Was this last meeting scientific? Do you want a science club?"

I watched their spirits wilt as they mentally weighed the questions. A deathlike silence followed my outburst. This is the end of the club, I thought.

Jack's hand hardly stirred the air as it went up timidly. I nodded recognition. "Madam Chairman."

"Jack."

"Madam Chairman," he repeated, "do you think the Marconian Club could put out its own science paper?"

Was he trying to divert my attention from "The Lion Tamer"? Was he rectifying the recent venture by a new and better one? I was baffled. Youth sometimes demands a swift transition of thought. The moderator problem was assuming vast proportions for me. Their recent failure prejudiced me. I could not visualize success in any of their plans. Yet, I reasoned, maybe they have learned their lesson and are anxious to prove it in another project.

"Your idea is good," I deliberated aloud. "When you have shown the faculty and student body that you can really make a science club work intelligently, you will be permitted one trial edition of a science paper."

The Marconians outdid themselves in their next three monthly programs. By April the club was functioning smoothly, intelligently and successfully. Since there would be only one more meeting that scholastic year, I thought it wise to allow the Marconians to put out their science paper in May.

Gathering material would not be so great a problem as the actual publication. All the juniors and seniors took typing. But the oversized enrollment and undersized accommodations, as well as the limited number of instructors, left little room for flexibility in the individual student's schedule for extracurricular typing. Burly football players vied with competent young ladies. The athletes' thumbs covered three keys and errors ran high. The girls, I feared, would realize that most of the presswork would fall to them and their enthusiasm would wane.

But the *Marconian News* was born amid piles of ruined dittos and under many hands discolored by "purple junk." There were editorials and articles provoking a friendly intellectual rivalry. It was a success.

One morning, while I was writing the outline for the first chemistry class on the blackboard, Bob's voice distracted me. There was a quality in his voice that I did not recognize. I turned just as he with a flourish slipped an envelope on my desk. "Look, Sister, what I got." It was a money order for the first prize from *Current Science*.

Current Science was a weekly publication of Tennessee State Teachers College and offered prizes for science articles. It encouraged participation in these contests by definite assignments.

The Marconian editor snatched such scoops. The publicity was good for Bob's scholastic morale. Every instructor liked Jim, his brother, and sympathized with his difficulty in learning. Only persistent endeavor maintained him a place in the classroom. No one ever suspected that Bob was secretly envious of the faculty's appreciation of his brother's efforts.

The *Current Science* first prize award gave Bob a greater interest in his studies. Coming up to Jim in class one day, Bob boasted, "I guess you know who's who now."

Such incidents only increased Jim's generosity. His noble spirit enclosed Bob's smaller self, perhaps forcing Bob to shape himself in his brother's pattern.

The Marconian Club was, during the war years, to have a rugged existence. But the club adjusted its activities to the times and survived. On one occasion, with characteristic enthusiasm, the members maneuvered an extracurricular patriotic program. It was a War Bond Rally. Its main feature was built on parodies of old songs that their parents loved. I, in thoughtless intrepidity, directed them. When the faculty attended the dress rehearsal, the first one to congratulate me was Sister Cecile, our organist, a member of a family of vocalists, herself renowned for her musical accomplishments. Only then did I realize my rashness in not asking her assistance. Too late I saw all the flaws that she would have removed.

The pastor attended opening night. His applause, he told the principal, was for the unrehearsed courtesy of the students toward their parents. Catching sight of a group of chaps roughing it in the yard the next day, he remarked to me, "Would you ever believe that they were the same gentlemen who last night helped the guests up and down the stage stairs to buy stamps and bonds?"

In a few years it was evident that the success of the club was no longer merely confined to science. It also helped fulfill the personality needs of many of its members. The students had occasion to share activities, to receive just compliments. Some were building friendships that later resulted in happy Catholic marriages. In class the students were more articulate; in the laboratory more alert.

At this point, I thought the students might be introduced to rotating experiments in their regular classwork. The technique had been highly recommended in the course in "Trends in the Teaching of Science" taken during college days.

The ordinary method used in the laboratory classes is to have all the students perform the same experiment at the same time. In the rotating method, material for about six different experiments is set out. The students are so grouped that each laboratory day they work out a different experiment and after six laboratory periods, the entire class has completed all the experiments. The procedure has an economic and an educational value. According to the common method, when all the students are working the same experiment, the laboratory has to be equipped to meet the needs of at least twenty-four students at one time. This means a large outlay for apparatus. From an educational point of view, the rotating method has the advantage of keeping students in contact with several types of apparatus for more than one laboratory class. In the single method the students see the apparatus once; then it is put away and other pieces are dispensed for their use. In the rotating method the students not only use the apparatus for their own experiment, but often assist others to assemble apparatus and to interpret and compare results. This impresses the type of apparatus, the experiment and the scientific phenomena on their minds more emphatically. The rotating method also gives students confidence in one another, makes them conscious of possible digressions in the use of apparatus and of the application of scientific principles. Although the rotating method allows more freedom to the students, it adds disciplinary problems.

The subject of atmospheric pressure and gas laws offered a series of excellent experiments for rotation. The lecture matter intrigued the students with the story of Otto von Guericke. Otto lived in the seventeenth century. He made one of the first recorded instruments for measuring air pressure, using a thirty-foot tube closed at one end, filled with water and inverted over a container of water. On top of this column of water, which extended above the roof of Otto's home, he placed a floating horned mannikin. The little devil ducked inside in stormy weather to reappear when sunshiny days were in the offing. My attempts at teaching the principles of atmospheric pressure made me wonder whether Sir Tempter didn't consider it the time to duck inside the classroom.

I remember a particular class in physics—the class of which Ray, Bob, Herman and Mary Jo were members—which had the knack of creating experiments of great moment. On one particular occasion I arranged the outlay of apparatus and surrendered the laboratory to my impractical and unpredictable class. Someone spilled the mercury out of the barometer tube, causing a skirmish for the elusive metal. About ten minutes after each group had finally begun its respective experiment, a most unnatural lull came over the class. I dropped a flask. No one even shuffled. But Mary Jo efficiently and silently cleaned away the debris. Ray, our gadget explorer, slipped the parts of a good Elgin into his shirt pocket. Herman was working admirably with a group of four students. Bob was recording data on the blackboard. It was as though someone had put the sign "Westinghouse Laboratories" on the outside of our building and they were playing the part.

I tried to recall what special prayers I had sent up that morning for patience and tact with my classes. The mystery cleared as the Reverend Superintendent ushered in and introduced the diocesan and state school supervisors. The students had seen them coming through the court to the laboratory!

I had often envied these inspectors the prestige which was powerful enough to discipline classes from a distance. The inspectors lost no time in becoming acquainted with the experiment of each group. I was relieved to notice the principal at the door. Good, I said to myself, now Sister Basil will direct them to another class.

But my hopes collapsed as I heard her address the inspectors, "Would you like to have Sister Jeremy assemble this group for a formal lecture?"

"No, no Sister. Let the class go right on." They stayed for the entire laboratory period during which the students showed themselves at their best—adept with apparatus and faithful in recording all data.

I was inarticulate as the inspectors thanked me courteously, commenting on the unusual alertness of the class and assuring me that the boys and girls were a promising group. From that day on, I determined the class would have to live up to its new reputation.

But lest such compliments threaten my humility, there were never lacking those incidents which make every teacher wonder whether skywriting might not be a more satisfying occupation. I remember once explaining that the barometer reading is not only due to the pressure of the miles of nitrogen, oxygen, carbon dioxide and the rare gasses in the air, but also to the water vapor in the air. A wee voice from the front row said faintly, "Is there water in the air, Sister?" I thought Mary Jo was trying to be funny. Although she had very little conception of scientific phenomena, I expected a student to have some idea of humidity.

Many in the class were shocked at such scientific ignorance. But here was a budding scientist, perhaps another Curie—who knows? Putting to the fore all my educational psychology, I tried to neutralize the charged atmosphere by kindness in my tone of voice.

"Yes, water in the vapor form is present in the air."

"How does the water get into the air, Sister?"

I thought that perhaps a question would arouse the dawning scientific attitude. "Where does the water go when it rains, Mary Jo?" I inquired.

Disgustingly the answer came, "Down the sewer and our cistern, Sister."

"But what about the large puddles that never reach the sewer?" I prodded.

"Oh, that! I never thought of that." But she was not satisfied. She still did not believe that there was moisture in the air. By this time the class was bored. But I had to go on.

"Did you ever notice moisture on the outside of a glass that was filled with cold water?" I continued.

"Oh, yes," she said. "But I could never figure how that water ever got on the other side of the glass when you poured it into the glass."

"That water on the outside of the glass is deposited by the moisture in the air when it hits the cold surface of the glass," I continued to explain.

"But why isn't Roosevelt all wet?" Triumphantly she pointed to the bust of the President on the history bookshelf.

Then, too, no matter how proficient a teacher may become in his own field, he must still admit to a certain incompetence in others. I was, however, quite abashed by an incident in one of the study periods I supervised daily. A forlorn little freshie was raising his hand. I walked up to his desk and whispered, "Need help, Steve?"

Flipping the pages of his literature, he complained, "Sister, I can't find who wrote Franklin's *Autobiography*."

Was this ignorance, or was he trying to act smart? Just then the boy in front of Steve, Jack's younger brother, Willie, whispered, "Don't ask her, Steve. She wouldn't know. Sister Jeremy just teaches science."

By December of that first year of World War II, there was a change in the atmosphere of the senior bungalow. Teaching became more difficult, though not less interesting. Some students, who hoped to benefit by the V-5 or V-12 programs, took a much more serious attitude toward their study of science. Others would be called by draft before the school year was over unless the principal was able to obtain a deferment for them. These, conversely, lagged in interest. Younger boys could look forward to but a few months of uncertain occupation after graduation until they, too, would be called. The girls were also influenced—there were farewells to brothers, fathers, sweethearts. We had tried to teach the students how to meet life, but this was an angle of life with which I had had no experience—war. Each student was more than ever an individual problem. I learned that war meant courage, loyalty, bravery, love and faith. We were to see ample proof of that in the sterling example of many of our heroic alumni. But war could also mean hate and sin and broken hearts. Day after day, week after week, I tried to show the students how to meet these gruesome war situations.

All too soon it was June again and valedictory time. Thank God I could not foresee the future or I could never have given such encouragement and hope to parents. Bob and Jim's parents came with the others to receive their soldier sons' diplomas. When the draft had called Jim in January, Bob insisted on going with his brother. The brothers had been sent on the same military mission. Jim was first to be reported missing in action, but later returned with a first-hand account of missing Bob's death. Jim had crawled to his brother as soon as he saw him fall. "Say good-by to Mom and Dad for me," Bob had gasped, "and tell Helen I love her."

"Sure, Bob," Jim promised choking, and started the act of contrition aloud. They went through it together to the end. Then Bob looked up at his brother, smiled and said weakly but still teasingly, "I guess you know who's who now."

Boys who had received no scholastic honor that graduation night returned after the war with purple hearts and medals. But most to be pitied were some graduates whom the war and its conditions had robbed of their heritage of Christian charity. A few came back soured by bitterness, others by hate and one by a complete loss of faith.

Hearing of these tragedies, I took comfort in the realization that ultimately every person is responsible for himself. The Divine Will is ever wise; it is the human will which determines what the final product will be: sanctity or sin. The sun is always the sun, but snow it melts and clay it hardens. Such abnormal times as war always underline our need for prayer, and we became more than usually conscious of our students and their families as we daily knelt before the Source of all light and strength.

Chapter Six

To those on the other side, the sight of Sisters produces varying impressions. The parishioners see us file in rank to and from church and get the idea of an army platoon. Where two are on a shopping tour, children still gaze in amazement, run to their mothers and tug at their skirts exclaiming, "Lookit, Mother, what are them? Pandas, penguins—what are they, Mother?" To the world in general, perhaps, we represent innumerable frustrated women, enduring day by day the drab martyrdom of cloistered confinement. None of these observers has felt the strong healthy pulse of community life.

There were twenty-eight of us at grand old St. Albert's. We ranged in age from eighteen to seventy-eight years. We were all Americans of various descents: German, Slav, French, Irish, Italian. In I.Q. we ranged from 100 up; in talents and skill we were adept in cooking, laundering, interior decorating and teaching all manner of subjects from the first to the twelfth grade. We were indeed a motley group of the Lord's servants, but a happy one. Servants—yes, this was what placed us in the category and gave us a common ground. We had all dedicated ourselves to serve others in a teaching community. As Sisters of St. Francis, we had vowed to observe the same rules and cherish the twin aims of our religious community: our own sanctification and the salvation of others through the education of youth. With all our idiosyncrasies and failings, we were enemies to the devil, the world and the flesh. Our alliance on these terms alone fostered an understanding for harmonious living. Yes, we called one another Sisters.

Feast days at St. Albert's were always impressive. Our novice mistress had often cited this parish as one noted for religious traditions. There we experienced to the full the beauty of living with the Church. Every great feast had scheduled at least one Solemn High Mass, sometimes two. The essentials of every Mass are the same, but rituals differ. The daily Low Mass, a half-hour period, fitted into our weekday routine. It made us realize the "alwaysness" of God—gave us strength, courage and peace on the shifting sands of our classrooms. There before the altar I daily renewed my offering of myself in God's service and caught again the spirit of my Profession: "All the days of my life in poverty, in chastity, and in obedience." I was in love then. I am still in love. An ordinary Sunday High Mass was solemn enough and recalled the commandment, "Remember, thou keep holy the Sabbath," and the majesty, justice and mercy of the Lord we served. But the Solemn High Mass, reserved for greater feast days, lifted our spirits still higher as the praises of the Triune God resounded through St. Albert's large Gothic Church. From the moment the three priests and their retinue of altar boys stepped into the Sanctuary until the final glorious "Holy, holy, holy Lord" of the men's choir, we lived eternity— God—Who was, Who is, and Who is to come, through and with and in His Son, Our Lord, Jesus Christ. Sunday mornings were thus devoted to enriching our own spiritual lives and in taking our parish and the whole world into our prayers. With opportunities to take part in four or even five Masses on any ordinary Sunday, we were certainly not spiritual paupers. This rich experience was one aspect of what our Divine Master meant by the "hundredfold" He would give for my consecration "All the days . . ."

Yet we are not all spirit. The body, too, had its times of relaxation and growth. October 4, the feast of our Holy Father St. Francis, was always a free day and for us at St. Albert's was like a little Christmas overflowing with true Franciscan joy. The preceding day is a fast day for Franciscans. On that day Sister Basil usually appointed several Sisters to help Sister Serene and Sister Marie in the kitchen so they too might share in the next day's festivities.

On October 3 Sister Martin and I were eagerly anticipating the next day's feast, on our way home from school. Suddenly she stopped and sniffed. "Sister Jeremy, do you smell what I do?"

"Oh, Sister Martin," I teased, "you smell just everything!" But as we peeked into the kitchen, rather to learn what was cooking than what our chores were, rich odors of chicken assailed our nostrils. Stooping over the oven, Sister Marie, flushed and perspiring, was gently turning golden pieces of chicken in a deep yellow juice.

Sister Martin gaped. "Why, Sister Marie, it's a fast day! We can't be having fried chicken tonight?"

"Go away—shoo!" Sister Marie reproved, fanning her apron at us. "Don't ask so many questions."

"All right, all right, never mind. I'll ask Sister Serene. She'll tell us. Come along, Sister."

But Sister Serene also knew how to keep a secret.

That evening at supper, after the usual spiritual reading, Sister Basil tapped the bell. "Sisters," she began, "Father O'Shea, as you all know, is director of Camp St. Joseph. He has invited us to spend our holiday there."

"Ohhh!" Little gasps of delight spiraled from all sides.

"Transportation will be provided. Our bulletin board will tell each of you what part you play in making the day a happy family gathering. *Benedicamus Domino.*"

"*Deo Gratias!*" we chorused with the opening of recreation. Sister Marie capped her ears with her hands but smiled gleefully as we exclaimed, "So that's why Sister Marie fried chicken on a fast day!"

Sister Martin and I were asked to serve breakfast at home and to plan the day's fun at camp. We planned our program right before night prayer. Sister Basil had no notion of what we might do but didn't seem to fear the risk.

"Sister Jeremy," said Sister Martin, beaming, "let's have a baseball game. We can divide the house into two teams. After that, we'll roller-skate. The older sisters will surely enjoy a whole afternoon of cards or bunco."

"Sounds perfect to me." And with that we set out for school to gather equipment—catcher's mitt, ball, bats, mask. "But, how about the roller skates?" I asked, while we packed a carton.

"That's easy." Sister Martin grinned. "You call Tom and Dave. They'll round up a dozen pairs."

Sister Martin and I dismissed Sisters Serene and Marie from the kitchen that evening—October 3. "We'll take over for breakfast right now," we offered. They had misgivings, but we prevailed. We had schemed a little surprise for the morning meal. First, we stripped the tables of their feast-day white cloths and substituted freshly laundered bed ticking. Then we put out old tin and crockery cups, found in an abandoned cupboard in the school basement. The bread we placed on the table in half loaves, to be broken as desired. We were sure St. Francis would have rejoiced in our poverty and gaiety. The Sisters came in after Mass. They gasped and viewed with various degrees of horror our barren board; at the kitchen sink, I giggled; Sister Martin could hardly keep her laughing inaudible. Just when Sister Basil, in complete consternation, was about to take action, Sister Martin and I zoomed out of the kitchen, carrying steaming platters of ham and eggs. Everyone caught the joke, and as Sister Ida read from the *Imitation*, the regular table service was taken from the drawers to receive the fresh pineapple, pecan rolls and coffee of the *real* breakfast.

Father O'Shea's bus transported our family of twenty-eight, our food supply, our baseball equipment and roller skates. We arrived at camp in a gay mood, and everyone enjoyed the informality of the picnic dinner. Later, when the food had been cleared away, Sister Martin called for the baseball game. We drafted Sister Marie, our cook, as one of our players.

"But I never played baseball, dears. In fact, I never saw a real baseball game."

"Come ooooonn," Sister Martin pleaded. "We'll show you how to play. Just follow our directions."

Sister Martin acted as umpire. I pitched. Sister Marie came up to bat. "Strike one . . . strike two." Sister Marie was hitting the air. Maybe a low one will help, I thought. "Strike three."

Sister Marie swung so hard she dropped the bat, lost her balance and sat sprawled in the dust. She picked herself up quickly, grabbed the bat and was ready for strike four. "Three strikes and you're out," called Sister Martin.

But Sister Marie stood immovable, gripping the bat for another pitch. "Sister Marie, you're out!" cried Sister Martin again. "Sister Cecile is coming to bat."

Sister Marie looked puzzled. "I don't see anything coming," she said. "If Sister Jeremy hasn't hit me yet, I don't think she will."

"But, Sister Marie," Sister Martin argued, coming up to her, "you had three strikes and you're out. Your turn at bat is up."

"Oh, no, Sister Martin," Sister Marie insisted, "you can't do that to me. You wanted me to play with you, and now you want me out. Oh, no! No, no! I'm here to stay."

"But I tell you, Sister Marie, the rules—the rules of the game! When you have three strikes, you're out."

"Strikes?" Sister Marie said blankly. "I did not strike anything yet."

Sister Martin threw up her hands and called, "O.K.! Sister Jeremy, you keep on pitching until Sister Marie strikes." The rest of the team took "time out" and sat on the grass. Finally, after innumerable pitches, Sister Marie got a hit. Everyone jumped up and shouted, "Hurrah for Sister Marie! Run, Sister Marie, run, run! You can make a homer on that hit. Hurry! Run!"

But Sister Marie stood frozen, overjoyed as she watched the ball soar almost out of sight, and then make its way down.

"Hurry, run, and you can make it a homer!"

"Run where?" Sister Marie finally asked.

"Over there," I yelled, pointing to first base. "At least make first base."

Sister Marie finally ran and got to first base before the ball bounced off the fielder's mitt. In the bleachers Sister Basil and Sister Serene were doubled up with laughter. "Sister Martin," called Sister Marie, "I often wondered when you remarked about people not getting to first base. So *this* is what you meant!" And she stamped up and down on the plate.

"Yes, Sister Marie. Now hold it!" the "fans" urged.

Already the second batter, Sister Cecile, stood at the plate. The first pitch should have been good for a double. It was. Everyone screamed, "Sister Marie, take second! Hurry! Here comes Sister Cecile to first."

Now Sister Marie was screaming, too. "What will I do with first? Oh, no! After all the yelling you did to get me to first base, I'm not moving."

Sister Martin called, "Game!"

"Oh, well," sighed the catcher, and she threw up her mitt. The game ended in the midst of hilarious laughing and chattering, as the other Sisters tried belatedly to give Sister Marie some idea of baseball.

"Let's roller-skate," I suggested a little later.

Sister Marie needed no coaxing. "Sister Jeremy," she begged, when we had reached the rink, "will you show me how to roller-skate?"

By this time I was fastening my own skates, and stared amazed at Sister Marie's venturesome spirit. If I knew my math she was in her fifties. I was about to help her put on a pair of skates when Sister Basil came up to us. "Sister Marie, you'd better not."

"Oh, please let her try, Sister Basil," I interceded.

"Sister *Mary* Jeremy, I cannot afford to have Sister Marie laid low with a broken leg. But I don't want to spoil your fun either. You may try one round; do be careful!"

"Thank you, Sister Basil," we both sang out.

"All right," I giggled, rising from my knees, "I'll hold you by the arm. Come along." I got her three fourths of the way up from the bench, when she slid helplessly to the floor, pulling me down with her. Sister Martin swung over from the other end of the pavilion and helped us both to our feet. Both of us instantly grabbed for Sister Marie, swaying on her way down to the floor again. Finally we put Sister Marie between us and held her by each arm. But she kept taking short, ladylike steps instead of the long glides of a skater. After about ten minutes Sister Marie remembered something important she wanted to talk over with Sister Basil and left us to our skating. "Thanks for the new experience," she chuckled and helped us remove her skates. "I'll try again at our next party."

Sister Martin and I joined the other Sisters who were circling the pavilion in pairs, smiling, chattering, and laughing merrily. When we were tired and hungry, we followed our noses and found Sister Marie, helping Sister Basil and the other nonskaters who were preparing juicy barbecued hamburgers.

Later, we chanted the Office of the Blessed Virgin in choir along the riverbank. Thus St. Francis himself in his Umbria must have sung praises to God and our Mother Mary. We knew he was approving—God's nature lover and troubadour that he was!

Next morning many of us limped to chapel. During meditation Sister Basil tapped me on the shoulder. I opened my eyes and whispered, "I wasn't sleeping." She smiled and whispered back, "Sister Jeremy, please see what happened to Sister Marie. She isn't here, and I noticed on my way to chapel that no breakfast has been started." I padded out of chapel.

"Sister Marie," I called over and over as I rapped at her door. Should I open it or go back to Sister Basil? A sudden thought came pell-mell: What if . . . no, it can't be! Never . . . Dear God, maybe we forced Sister Marie to overdo it. Maybe she's had a heart attack. . . . I didn't savor the idea of shaking the dead but what should I tell Sister Basil? Reluctantly, I tiptoed into Sister Marie's room. To my great relief I saw her breathing—the deep, deep breathing of a sound sleep. I shook her gently.

"Mmmmm, I'm out? How can I be out?" she mumbled, half-conscious.

"Sister Marie! Sister! Wake up! It's almost six o'clock!"

"Huh?" And one blue eye shot open. "Oh? Wha—? Sister Jeremy! Did I oversleep?" She made a sudden jerk to get up but fell back with a groan. "Oh, dear Lord! I think I've had a stroke. I can't move!"

"No, you haven't a stroke," corrected Sister Basil, who was now standing in the open doorway. "Sister Marie, you stay in till your muscles recover from yesterday's exercise. Sister Martin and Sister Jeremy will take over your duties."

I took a deep breath and mentally dusted off my high school home economics course.

Next day Sister Martin and I prevailed on Sister Serene to let us prepare chop suey. Sister Ida came in to prepare vegetables. Just before serving, Sister Martin lifted the lid over the concoction. "This smells powerful," she sniffed pouring in salt. "I bet none of you salted it."

"I did," announced Sister Serene calmly.

"I did," added Sister Ida.

"I did." I glared.

At supper the six water pots of Cana would have done us good service. The meal had hardly begun when Sister Basil told Sister Martin, "Sister, we have no water." After filling our pitchers several times during the remainder of the meal, Sister Martin remarked, rouguishly, "Sisters in Christ, after all, Saint Francis put ashes on his food to make it less delectable."

"Yes," I comforted with mock solemnity, "salt is more soluble and digestible than ashes."

And so week followed week and year succeeded year at St. Albert's. Each August a few familiar faces were missing from our staff, and new ones took their places.

Naturally it was hard to part with co-educators who had gone through the mill and were always ready to meet a fellow Sister half-way. Farewells to close companions who shared all the sunlight and shadows of our community living were tolerable only because of our realization of being in the service of the Great King all the days ...

The same year that Sister Martin was assigned to St. Theresa's in Downing, Sister Ida became head of the chemistry department at Padua College in Tannerton.

Sister Martin, always ready with a joke, a trick and a laugh; Sister Ida, with a solution to any scholastic problem—neither would grace our family circle this year. My tears were quite profuse. The first few weeks of their absence from St. Albert's I would expect Sister Martin to pop out of any corner most any time. More than once upon stating a problem I caught myself wondering why Sister Ida wasn't offering a solution. Nevertheless, I felt myself gradually maturing spiritually. "Detachment from creatures is nothing else than attachment to God," I pondered. I learned to share my joys and tears ever more deeply with Christ, my divine Spouse. And it seemed that, in true Franciscan fashion, "My God" was becoming more and more "My All." Yes, "all the days of my life" I wanted to love Him.

It was not long after one of these annual changes in personnel that Sister Patrick, a newcomer to St. Albert's, and I were doing the Saturday morning shopping. To provide continued wholesome food, it was more economical to shop at the large supermarkets. Now with market baskets over our arms, shawls pulled tightly over heads and shoulders, we directed our course toward the Fifth Avenue market.

"Sister Patrick," I said on the way, "let's survey the stalls first before we make any purchases."

Agreeably Sister Patrick smiled at each vendor as we looked at their products. Conquered merchants would put a head of cabbage in her empty basket, potatoes, other vegetables. They thought we were the Little Sisters of the Poor, whose rule necessitated them to beg food for themselves and their poor.

Every excursion with Sister Patrick afforded pleasant surprises. Sister reveled in pushing the wire basket up and down the aisles while I selected the purchases. On one such occasion, as I was examining a head of lettuce, a short, gray-haired woman approached us.

"Pardon me, Sisters. My name is Mrs. Muelleman. I'm not a Catholic, but I feel close to the Sisters ever since they were so wonderful to Mr. Muelleman in the hospital—especially Sister Pancratius. You know Sister Pancratius at St. Anthony's?"

"No, I'm afraid we don't."

Our new acquaintance was undaunted. "Anyhow, with Christmas just two weeks away I said to myself, 'Hattie, what are you going to get Sister Pancratius for Christmas?' And just like that I thought of it. Four Roses! What could be more festive than Four Roses? But on second thought, I really don't know much about the Sisters and I was just wondering . . . Tell me, what do you think, Sisters?"

While I mentally estimated the per cent ethanol, Sister Patrick beamed enthusiastically. "Why, 'twould be a lovely gift!"

Mrs. Muelleman's eyes brightened. "You think it would be all right? You think Four Roses would be appropriate for a nun? And would her superior allow her to accept it?"

"Sure an' faith, Mrs. Muelleman." Sister Patrick smiled reassuringly. "Sister Pancratius could offer your gift to St. Joseph—that is, if she has special devotion to St. Joseph—or to St. Anthony."

I stared open-mouthed at my glib companion.

Mrs. Muelleman drew a deep breath of relief. "Thank you so much, Sisters. Merry Christmas!" And she trudged along.

"Sister . . ." I began.

But Sister Patrick sighed. "Poor thing! Four roses. Why just *four* roses? Bless her heart. Maybe she couldn't afford a dozen."

"Sister Patrick, you don't . . ."

" 'Tis a sweet thought though," my companion interrupted. "And after all, 'tis the thought that counts."

"Yes," I agreed, giving up, " 'tis the thought that counts."

This was only one of my experiences with Sister Patrick's often ludicrous simplicity and naïveté. If our Franciscan family were to parallel the contemporary associates of our Holy Father, St. Francis, Sister Patrick could have well been our Brother Juniper, the early companion of St. Francis. She succeeded Sister Martin in second grade, and so inherited the coveted duty of preparing the little ones for First Holy Communion.

Early one fine Saturday morning in April I looked out the community room window to see her forming her class ranks in the courtyard. That day her First Communicants were to receive the Sacrament of Penance for the first time. Five minutes later Sister Rufina, going to the window sill to sharpen a pencil, noticed a commotion outside. "Sister Basil, why are all the second graders huddled over at the side of the building? I thought they were going to Confession."

Sister Basil walked over and looked out too. "Dear me, there seems to be some sort of confusion. I don't see Sister Patrick at all. Sister Jeremy, will you please investigate?"

Sniffing mystery, excitement and adventure, I dashed out and almost collided with Father Sullivan at the sacristy door. I bowed apologetically. "Sister, aren't they coming in? Where's Sister Patrick?" he asked.

With that, the children turned and shouted, "Over here, Father!"

We went to the huddle to see Sister Patrick steadying herself on a heap of shifting coal. Pete, the janitor, had neglected to close the chute.

"Sure an' how's a body to kaip eyes on the little ones and on coal chutes besides?" she queried, on firm ground again. She brushed off her habit and straightened her veil.

Sister Damian, another newcomer, also provided many a chuckle. One evening during recreation Sister Damian, busily treading the sewing machine next to Sister Robert, asked, "Will you go with me to the dentist tomorrow, Sister Robert?"

"Gladly. What time?"

"About three-fifteen. You know, Dr. Thornton wants to extract my upper teeth next week. He claims the enamel is cracked from biting thread when I sew."

There was a lull in the surrounding conversation and a few snickers as Sister Damian remonstrated, "I never bite thread."

We all looked up just in time to see her stop the machine, remove the cloth from under the needle and proceed to bite the dangling thread. "Oh, yes, you do!" we chorused, laughing. Sister Damian sat stunned.

"Never mind," Sister Robert consoled, patting her shoulder. "We love you just the same!"

Yes, love was the pattern. Love was the warp and woof of our lives. Daily the verse of the Psalm, "Behold, how good it is and how pleasant for brethren to dwell together in unity," became more meaningful. Oh, there were disagreements now and then, and sometimes a sharp retort and a little gossip too. But a deep mutual charity welled from our hearts and flavored our whole existence almost as perceptibly as the familiar odors that met our senses through the year. In August and September, neighborhood kitchens and St. Albert's exuded mouth-watering aromas of brewing ketchup, corn salad, pickles, canned peaches, applesauce and grape jelly; the community room smelled of new books, freshly shined shoes and the fumes of hectograph ink. On holidays and holy days—October 4, All Saints Day, Thanksgiving, Christmas—St. Albert's was diffused with tantalizing odors of fruit and mince pies, savory roast fowl, the fragrance of incense, the turpentine of evergreens, the clean odor of scrubbed and waxed floors. Lent, Good Friday, Easter brought with them the scent of freshly painted walls, varnished floors, ammoniated window water, starched curtains, Easter egg dyes. May and June always carried the sweet air of lilacs and lilies of the valley on the altars, and the warm woolly smell of habits being pressed, of the winter shawls being wrapped in mothballs.

Thus did the homeyness and camaraderie of St. Albert's season "all the days" with peace and joy and enthusiasm in living for God.

Chapter Seven

"No, Sister Martin. For the millionth time, no!"

It was summer again at Tannerton and Sister Martin and I were having a round of ping-pong in the college gym the evening before summer school started. "Sister Jeremy, do you have to be like that? I can see you have a secret. Important like, maybe? Mother Regina did send for you today, didn't she?"

"Yes, Sister Mary Martin." I ducked under the table to retrieve the ball.

"Don't Mary Martin me. I think you're horrid!" My partner gave the next serve a resounding "thwack!"

"Try to understand, Sister. What Mother Regina told me was personal; I was asked not to discuss it until after appointments on August 12."

"Well, you don't have to tell me right out. Let me guess," she pleaded.

"No use. I'll just say no to everything."

"Oh, keep your old secret."

Yes, I did keep the secret. On the way to night prayer I reviewed the events of the last few days.

Every June as I dusted each piece of apparatus and placed it carefully away, I recalled the words of Eugene Field's poem: "Now don't you move 'til I come, he said." A feeling of uneasiness usually came over me, lest in the fall it would be another's privilege to find them there, even if by then "covered with dust." Each spring the students' inevitable question, "Sister, are you coming back in September?" had to be answered with the same simple, honest, "I don't know."

Although a Sister's obedience requires her to accept a new duty willingly, it does not prescribe joy at leaving a cherished old one.

My own anxiety about a new duty was always assuaged by the thought of a stimulating and refreshing summer session among my great family of Sisters at our Alma Mater. The Sisters who had their bachelor's degrees were registered as special students. Such sweet serenity! No longer were we plagued with required courses. We chose subjects immediately or remotely related to our teaching. There was a wide variety, such as religion, education, science, mathematics, philosophy, English or languages. Thus our study broadened and enriched our educational development and prepared us better for the classroom in September.

The day I arrived, Mother Regina's summons disturbed me not at all. I merely wondered what little side duty on campus she would assign me. I was wholly unprepared for the bolt of lightning that zigzagged before me when she announced, "Sister Jeremy, we are taking you off the teaching staff."

I almost stopped breathing. Had I heard aright? Off the teaching staff? Was I to be assigned to the kitchen? Snatches of my novitiate instructions—"Every work done in obedience is pleasing to God . . . The obedient man shall speak of victory . . . The perfect practice of obedience offers the greatest challenge to human nature"— echoed in my mind. Above them all I heard my own heart struggling to say, "Thy Will be done," as Mother Regina explained, "As you know, Sister Ida, the head of the college chemistry department is not too well. Also classes are getting larger, and there are more of them."

Well, I thought, so that's it. The joy of again assisting Sister Ida lessened the pain of parting from St. Albert's. Visions of "lab boy" floated before me. I saw myself checking and dispensing apparatus and chemicals, with opportunities for refreshing my undergraduate chemistry, covered with the rust of years. Not too bad, I observed.

But then came the thunderclap: "Sister, you are to be in residence at the University of Illinois."

As over falling water, from a high mountain, I heard the rest. "We want you to obtain your master's degree and a doctorate in chemistry. Although appointments will not be announced till August 12, I wanted you to know this so you could brush up on your German and French. I would prefer your not discussing this matter with anyone before the official date."

Dazed, I stumbled out of Mother's office, sagging under the weight of my new obedience. I had to tell Someone. I found myself on my knees in chapel, later than usual saying, "Dear God, I can't do it. Why not someone else? There's Sister Hyacinth, another chem major and far more brilliant than I. Yet my own grades were always good. But a state university! I'll fail the first examination! No—I can't go. Why, I never was in such an environment. I never attended any but a Catholic college. I'll simply tell Mother Regina. No, I can't do it!" On and on my vigorous self-will raced! How long I stayed there I don't remember. But calm came at last, and I could finally say, "Thy Will be done" and smile again at the tabernacle. "But help me, Lord Jesus," I entreated as the enormity of the task towered before me.

That night I fell asleep praying to Sister Olivia for a measure of her serenity.

Now if only Sister Martin would stop pestering me, I could perhaps relegate my secret obedience and concentrate on my summer subjects. I *did* want to see God's Will in this unexpected assignment for me—a nobody in His service. I *did* want to be of maximum use to the community that had accepted, mothered and educated me through the years. Of course I wanted our college science department to be able to give its students nothing but the best. Only one little demon of rebellion tormented my subconscious with, "Why does it have to be *me?*"

The university fall session was many weeks away. Classes would begin in October. Our registrar sent a transcript of my credits. By return mail its graduate office informed me that I was accepted in the graduate school. Also that an applicant for the advanced degree in chemistry was required to take a twelve-hour written entrance examination in the four fundamental fields of chemistry. Finally that no student was allowed to acquire residence toward the second year of graduate study for the doctorate until he had passed satisfactorily the two-hour examinations in French and German.

Vacation days were over. Twelve hours written, three hours in

127

each field of chemistry—inorganic three, analytical three, organic three, physical three—almost as long a list as the Biblical forty-thousand signed of the Tribe of Judah, of the tribe of Benjamin, of the tribe of . . . I had never taken physical chemistry. That would be the first washout and a prerequisite to be fulfilled if I was to remain in the department of chemistry. I had but one foot in the corridor of the graduate school of a state university's chemistry department. I stood there holding an empty bag, it seemed to me. Thus far my own teaching experience was limited to high school chemistry. Theoretical undergraduate chemistry had become dimmed with the years. Twelve hours was four times as much as I would need to express my remaining chemical knowledge. Probably one round of the clock's second hand would do it. As soon as the college summer session closed, I determined to put my nose to the grindstone.

The day after appointments the court teemed with taxis. Sisters were collecting baggage and grouping themselves according to the various missions. Mother Regina, always a Mother, went from one to the other with a word, a smile, a handshake, a blessing.

Sister Bonaventure, Sister Ida and I had joined the St. Albert's group. "Sister Jeremy," Sister Ida teased, "what happened to the *five cent* taxis?"

"Your memory!" I squirmed with a grin.

Other groups turned toward us, wondering what had caused the loud laughter.

Sister Patrick hummed, "I'll Take You Home Again, Kathleen" as she bade me good-by, adding, "What'll we tell Pete, Sr., for you?" I nodded wordlessly, waved and swallowed the old lump. As their taxi whizzed out of the grounds, I called, " 'By, all of you, and pray for me. I'll miss you and dear old St. Albert's."

"Do you think we'll do, Sister Ida?" asked Sister Bonaventure, seeing my brimming eyes. I wiped away the tears and turned on a smile for them.

"You'll be my mainstay till I leave for the university, but then I'll need you more than ever." My voice quivered.

Together we walked inside.

Six weeks were left—six solid weeks. I crammed every day, every hour, every minute. But I seemed to know less and less, and hourly the mountain to be scaled towered higher before me. As the deadline drew near, my nostalgia grew, threatening to nullify my ability to assimilate knowledge.

The desk at the window of the library history stacks offered seclusion but it was soon a torture chamber, for, from the window, gusts of loneliness befuddled me. The Sisters assigned to teach at the Academy constantly bustled by on the broad walk below, bubbling talk of subjects and students. To me they were not Tannerton teachers, but my Sisters across the plains of Indiana into Ohio. Printed chemical terminology blurred, and my ink-written notes ran together.

One hot afternoon there was a knock at the door. I stuffed my hankie into my pocket and in a shaky voice called, "Ave."

"How is every little thing, Sister Jeremy?" greeted Sister Ida, as she stepped into the stack room and rested one hand on the pile of chemistry books before me. With the other she held out a cool glass of Seven-Up.

"I couldn't say," I mumbled. I was sure now it was because of Sister Ida that I had been transferred from St. Albert's. My Guardian Angel kept shouting in my ear, "Obedience is homage to God." Then I looked at Sister Ida's face, drawn with pain and worn with heavy duties of directing a major and large department in an undergraduate college. I repented, "Thanks, Sister." I took the drink.

"Sister Jeremy, you're homesick not so much for St. Albert's, but for any classroom. Let's take a stroll."

Sister Ida was not the only one who sympathized with my inner conflict. At recreation I became more acquainted with my future confreres on the college staff. They welcomed me warmly, and gradually my feeling of aloneness dropped away. "We made it, Sister Jeremy," they encouraged. "You will too." Even before I left, I began to inhale a little of that same good old family spirit I had so loved at St. Albert's.

My appointment took on the proportions of a community project. Sister Elsa, my new superior, arranged to have the novices clean and press my habits and veils while I devoted all my time to study.

Regulation creases were sharp, and I hoped they would cleave through the dense forest of scientific ignorance in which I was groping. This was to be another solo flight. Sister Hugh, who was to be my companion on the university campus, was majoring in French Literature.

As departure day drew nearer, Sister Ligouri from St. Michael's Home offered us transportation by car. Sister Edgar, German professor at the college, was working on her thesis. This was a golden opportunity for her to use the university library stacks.

Good old convent court! Another good-by scene after breakfast.

"What's this?" I stared in amazement as the car from the Home lurched to a stop before our luggage.

"Hi, Sister Jeremy!" the driver called.

"Why, little Joe Buda!" I gasped, as a six-footer pulled himself out of the front seat.

"You remember me!" he beamed. "How do you like my new car, Sister? Glad to give you a ride. Hope it holds together. Just got the last part yesterday in the junk yards on 66."

Since the trunk section was limited, to use a temperate expression, Sister Hugh and I sandwiched part of the luggage between us. Our flowing habits filled in space like paper packing and kept the assembly from rattling. We were stationary. As we approached the sweltering and humid town, we felt like cupfuls of jello trying to remain firm at 98°F and 95 per cent relative humidity. My creases! I was hoping my veil would still show some signs of having been pressed. It did. I had added countless little creases en route.

Sister Hugh and I bade good-by to our escorts at the graduate office. The secretary, a Miss Vogt, efficiency itself, directed, "Fill this out," and handed each of us what looked like a round-trip ticket to India. We sat at a near-by table struggling with the five-foot form of four by six cards separated by perforations. Sister Hugh had filled them out before, and as soon as she had completed hers, helped me to decipher the directions on mine.

Miss Vogt went on directing her staff, oblivious of us. Finally I presented my forms, "Sister Jeremy," she clipped out in her high-pitched voice, as she scrutinized the cards, "your transcript did not include advanced calculus. You can't take this course in physical chemistry as you have indicated unless you fulfill this prerequisite."

"But that's my minor," I objected. "Don't I have to carry it parallel?"

"Sister Jeremy, our job is to see that you have proper sequence. Moreover, as stated on the cards, you must see each professor before being allowed into his class. I advise you to see Professor Reynolds immediately. Possibly he may let you parallel the calculus with the physical chemistry. Without his signature we can't allow such a privilege."

I crossed the campus to the chemistry building, consulted the directory, and found Professor Reynolds' name emblazoned in large letters on one of the doors. A tall, blue-eyed man in a laboratory smock resembling Swiss cheese in color and holes answered my persistent knock. "I would like to talk to Professor Reynolds," I ventured.

"Professor Reynolds is not in," came the curt reply.

The next day I returned with the same problem to the same formidable door. This time the door was open. A man was seated at the desk, gazing out of the window—smockless—bearing a great resemblance to the man I had seen the day before. When I rapped, he continued looking out of the window and sort of grunted, "Yes?"

Surmising this to be Professor Reynolds, I addressed him and presented my problem. He never turned once from the window. Sternly he commanded, "You will register for advanced calculus." Physical chemistry was deferred.

The first day of examinations changed my status from a high school science teacher's to that of a graduate student's at a state university. I had thought I knew the formula for water, for table salt and for similar simple chemical compounds. Now everything was confused; I was tense, fearful, terrified, numb. The atmosphere of the university chemistry department should never be contaminated with chemical heresy. Yet, I felt, here I was, writing just that. I wondered vaguely if I would awake from this bad dream and find myself a happy high school science teacher again, or was

131

this purgatory? Oh, the tricks of homesickness! Sister Hugh, my one and only link with home, tried to comfort me but my sense of incompetence frequently elicited letters to Mother Regina in the following vein:

University of Illinois
November 17, 1944

DEAR MOTHER REGINA,

You have been receiving weekly reports of my regression in chemistry. I feel that it is only fair to you and the community to state that I cannot make the grade, and to ask to be removed from this field of work before the community is disgraced by my dismissal.

Recommending myself to your kind prayers and those of the community, I am

Respectfully yours,
SISTER MARY JEREMY

Invariably, forty-eight hours later I received the same answer:

Mother house
Tannerton

DEAR SISTER JEREMY,

The obedient soul speaks of victory. A community of 700 is with you. You will make good.

Devotedly,
MOTHER M. REGINA, O.S.F.

The time between classes I spent in the chemistry library. The first time I entered, all heads came up from their books. Some students gasped; others stared. I rechecked regulations: rosary in place, knots of my cord on the right side and properly spaced, my crucifix hanging at the proper length, my veil straight. And then it dawned. This was not a Catholic atmosphere. These students probably had never seen Sisters. At least they had never seen Sisters on the University of Illinois campus, and hardly in a chemistry department. For them I might have fallen out of Chaucer's *Canterbury Tales.*

I changed my tactics and used the chemistry library only when the intermissions between classes were lengthy. For the ten-minute intervals I found a room in a dark corner of the main floor. It was labeled CHEMISTRY MUSEUM. Student lockers lined the corridor on either side of the open door. One day as a student closed his locker, he turned and faced the room. He gaped without a word. His surprised expression was a mixture of amazement and incredulity. He might well have regarded me a live specimen among the chemical curiosities.

Our university class in organic preparations numbered about ninety. The first day before class a student bravely accosted me and in the usual friendly campus fashion, greeted me, "Hello, ma'am, are you registered for this course, too?"

"Yes, sir," I answered politely.

"Well, ma'am, can you remove any of the uniform?" he inquired courteously. His manner precluded any hint of boldness. Accustomed as I was to the questions of high school boys and girls, I tried to have patience with this child of an older growth.

"But are you going to work the experiments?" he persisted.

"Of course." How did he expect me to get a credit for a laboratory course without working the experiments? He went away, evidently wondering how anyone could work efficiently in such full sleeves and flowing veil as mine. He had something there. It really is an art.

This same young man, Mr. Britt, later proved a good friend. He often helped by suggesting short cuts in laboratory procedures. But for a long time he would not call me *Sister*. He said he loved his own sisters so much that he could never give any other woman that designation. I appreciated his tribute to his sisters, while he kept on "yes, ma'am-ing" me. But one day he had set up an intricate organic apparatus extending about eight feet horizontally and four feet vertically. He was just about to begin the reaction in the first chamber when something gave way and the entire setup took on a Tower-of-Pisa look. He was desperate. "Sister! Sister Jeremy," he called, "hold this thing, please!" After that day Mr. Britt always called me "Sister." He still does!

The first semester was soon well under way. Sister Hugh dragged

133

her many large and small books of De Musset, Lamartine and De Vigny to our room each night and periodically helped me review my French. Her own research into the critical articles published in *Moniteur Universel* from 1813 to 1837 kept pace with my laborious assignments. We rose early and attended Mass in the Newman Club center. Our morning prayers said, we separated till noon when we met for lunch served in the Home Economics division. The hot plate Sister Elsa had provided saw many a little urn of black coffee and saucepan of bouillon soup as we pored over books and notes.

"Organic Preps" was an excellent course for increasing the number and size of corns and calluses, and not bad for developing fallen arches either. In the appendix of the laboratory manual was a very helpful table which indicated by columns how much time it took for every step in every experiment. For assembling apparatus, for example, one half hour; for agitating chemicals, fifteen minutes; for adding, drop by drop, concentrated acid, one hour; for reflux, one to two hours; and so on, to the final crystallization of the purified product. In all, as listed, most of the experiments were not to take more than one or two days. But this time element, I soon found, was a very unrealistic fancy of a scientific visionary. The specifications should have been raised to some mathematical power, or belonged to the category of arithmetic or geometric progressions. The time actually consumed in such experiments amounted to days, sometimes weeks.

The yield or product prepared we submitted to the instructor, with laboratory notes. Our final grade depended almost entirely on the quantity and purity of the yield. Whether I overpurified the material or failed in proper technique, I never knew; what I did know was that I could never obtain much in the matter of a yield. I also knew my final grade would be very low unless I could get some outstanding results for the remaining preparations, and this was mid-semester! The next synthesis just had to be superior, I determined.

I followed directions in the laboratory manual, meticulously raising the allowed time for everything to the proper number of days and weeks. After long dogged work, I admired a batch of beautiful white crystals in their last wash in a flask. I poked at them with a stirring rod—my crystals had shrunken to a sampler, nearly microscopic. My head spun. My heart thumped. My feet were getting cold. I grabbed the lab table, looked down and sighed in relief. Thousands of little pink crystals smiled up at me from my laboratory apron, my shoes and the floor. As I looked, I saw the hole I had poked in the bottom of the flask. With one scoop of the laboratory towel, I picked up the mass of crystals from the surroundings, placed towel and crystals in a large evaporating dish, washed the crystals off the towel, and recrystallized. The yield merited an "A."

Our research problems were usually intriguing and tantalizing. But the bright ideas that took form at dawn seldom, if ever, materialized by dusk. Other students could work in the laboratories until wee hours, but our religious rule required Sisters to be off the campus by six o'clock ordinarily. It was only on rare occasions that we attended an evening lecture.

One afternoon during a tedious class which ended at five, a bright idea struck me about the research problem I had been drooping over for days. I dashed out of class and up to the laboratory and worked until the university clock chimed six. As I pulled off my laboratory apron and surveyed the room for burning gas jets and running water, I noticed that a large stock bottle of concentrated sulfuric acid had not been returned to the store room. Hurriedly I picked it up on my way out of the building. As I did so, the bottom fell out—and so did the bottom of my habit. There was nothing else to do now but wait until after dark. How I got to our residence five blocks from the chemistry building without being observed, I don't know. But no one ever mentioned seeing a creature in a brown wool, modified ballerina scurrying along the twilight lanes. I often wondered if the students thought it was an evening variation of our garb.

Obviously we Sisters were a curiosity on the campus. For two years we were the only Sisters there. Even Catholic students did not know too much about us. I had thought all Catholics knew that Religious Orders of women are devoted to special corporal or spiritual works of mercy, and that their habits vary. Sister Hugh and I had the hardest time explaining that color or pattern has nothing to do with status in the Order or rank in the Church, where the Sisters are concerned; that we did not transfer from one community to another at will; and that we did *not* know every Sister in every Order in the United States. Religious stand in the same relation to one another as a Navy man to an Army man or a Marine.

Our garb did cause some amusing situations, though. Anyone who has ever been on a university campus for home-coming football season, knows the artistry displayed at the various fraternity and sorority houses. To satisfy our curiosity on one occasion Sister Hugh and I made a tour of the various houses to view their decorations. One fraternity had erected a very colorful Indian village. As we were admiring the project, a gentleman came up and asked, "Pardon me, ladies, but would you please tell me what part you represent in this pageant?" We probably looked to him like the missionaries sent to bring Christianity to the natives.

My own religious conversion, too, was the goal of a few well-meaning students. Mr. Chambers, a zealous Latter-day Saint, tried to convince me that I could still be saved. His wife, he said, was saved when she was twenty-five. This was quite complimentary. It had been more than a few years since I had been twenty-five myself.

One of the requirements for Masters of Science in chemistry was to attend the science seminar, take part in the discussions and give a paper on a current theoretical problem. The discussions from my lecture chair in the classroom were not too bad. But the theoretical paper floored me. I stood in the footlight glare, frightened. It never occurred to me that many students might come away with only meager knowledge of my report findings but a great deal of knowledge about the intricacies of my religious outfit. It was not rare for a student to be teasingly heckled while delivering his report. My audience, to my great relief, was most courteous, and their well-put questions were not nearly so difficult as I anticipated.

Refreshments were always served at such seminars. Members of the class rotated as hosts or hostess. (I was the only woman in the class.) The day that Mr. Britt and I were serving, Mrs. Dominelli, the housemother, decided on a surprisingly "different" menu—chili con carne. Preparations were grand. Mrs. Dominelli, a vigorous woman in her early fifties, ceremoniously ground, mixed, spiced and cooked the six pounds of beef, kidney beans and divers savory ingredients. All her large kettles filled, she bustled from one to another keeping the contents in agitation. Mr. Britt and another student called for the steaming mixture and paraded up the backsteps of the chemistry building, each with a large kettle. The aroma may not have blended amiably with the acrid fumes of chemicals, but it certainly did add a homey touch. I had fifty beakers lined up, but no service to convey this semi-solid. I checked fifty new porcelain spatulas from the store room. Embarrassed, I watched the group of students and professors trying to eat what chili they could rescue via spatula. What good material for a sound movie or television!

After three semesters, I obtained my master's degree. Sister Hugh and I decided to celebrate. Our little country school mission of Cloverville was only thirteen miles west. Friday afternoon of the week end between semesters we caught a jitney and were soon bumping along. I never suspected that Sister Hugh had phoned the Sisters three days before, announcing the happy news of my graduation. On our arrival the three of them stood on the tiny porch singing, "Congratulations to you!"

My place at the table was decorated with a figurine of a graduate, deftly fashioned of pipe cleaner and crepe paper. Beside the plate lay a beribboned scroll. Great was our merriment as I read the "official" document, inscribed in beautiful script:

This is to certify that
SISTER MARY JEREMY, O.S.F.

having satisfactorily survived the corns, bunions and calluses induced by prolonged standing at lab tables and having absorbed her quota of chemical fumes, is herewith granted the degree of M.B.B. (Master of Beaker Breakers), duly presented by this fully accredited institution on this third day of February, A.D., 1946.

[Signed]
J. NELSON PICKLEPACKER, *Pres.*

How well my Sisters appreciated my ordeal!

Three days later a tiny note from Mother Regina found its way to my mailbox:

Mother house
Tannerton
February 5, 1946

DEAR SISTER JEREMY,

Congratulations! We're all proud of you. "The obedient soul shall speak of victory."

As always,
MOTHER M. REGINA, O.S.F.

The next big hurdle was the Ph.D. I still had to struggle over the minors of physical chemistry and physics. Additional requirements included a two-hour written examination in French and in German; six hours written and three hours oral in major and minor fields; and the final hurdle to leap—the defense of the thesis, the subject of which was barely embryonic.

By June the French hurdle was behind me. The summer faced me with thermodynamics and nuclear chemistry since there would be a conflict in schedule the following term. The German examination was to be in October. A few days before the summer session I had my laboratory research desk covered with references for the courses, a German dictionary and a few German chemistry books. I was sorting these and arranging them on a book rack one day when Mr. Britt sauntered into the laboratory exclaiming, "Look at my schedule—an education course on problem children. This will give me two units and that's all I need for my minor. What are you taking this summer, Sister Jeremy?"

"Thermodynamics and nuclear chemistry, with chemical German as a sideline."

Mr. Britt slumped into a chair and began fanning himself.

"What's the matter? Are you dizzy?" I questioned with real concern.

"Sister Jeremy, it's you who are dizzy, or on the way to becoming a psychopath."

I didn't know it then, but after two weeks of summer school, I realized Mr. Britt was right when he doubted my rationality. With God's help I made a "B" in thermodynamics and an "A" in nuclear. But the German hurdle was still ahead, and French verbs kept confusing my German forms. I remembered Red and thanked the Lord for having taught fundamental German. The French scientific vocabulary is very similar to the English. Perhaps it would be better to say that both languages use the Latin and Greek roots for most of their scientific terminology. But the Germans are as exclusive as Caesar's, "All Gaul is divided into three parts, etc." Their scientific vocabulary is indeed foreign. From the close of summer session in August to the beginning of the fall term in late September, I spent about eight hours a day translating German chemical journals. Yet all this was not enough to give me confidence.

It was only the blessing of obedience that kept me smiling and optimistic. St. Jude, the saint of impossible cases, was the one whom I invoked to put some scientific German into my brain cells and let it simmer there. Good St. Jude! After classes began in September there was very little time for extra German, and the date of the examination was galloping toward me. If this had been a personal matter, it would not have upset me as it did, but I represented a community of religious teachers. Our institutions had "A" ratings with the state universities and educational accrediting associations wherever we were established. I could not let the community down. That was the crux of the situation. I don't know whether I prayed more than I studied, but I do know that I did both as well as I could.

I had the habit of going to the chemistry library daily to pick up a German journal at random, translating as much as I could. Then, with recourse to a dictionary, I would fill in the many blanks.

The examination in German was scheduled from seven to nine one evening in early October. At 6:55 I presented myself in the chemistry building. "Sister Jeremy," the proctor called.

I stepped to the desk to receive the books marked with the German articles I was required to translate. My hand trembled. I took the book and could hardly get back to my place. I opened to the page indicated. Tears welled in my eyes. There it was—the article that I had translated in the library that very afternoon. I sat there thanking God and St. Jude and recalling the advice of Mother Regina, "The obedient soul shall speak of victory."

God was very good, and my feeble efforts were rewarded. The professors were the personification of kindness. Comprehensives, both oral and written, were over in June of that year and I was looking forward to being off the campus by the end of August. That would depend on whether or not the research problem took satisfactory shape by then and was accepted by the major professors.

Again St. Jude came through. My laboratory work I completed by mid-August. All that remained was the thesis and its defense. Happily Sister Hugh had also fulfilled her last requirements. Thus, after four years of study, we returned home to Tannerton. My new family of Sisters at the college heartily welcomed me to the faculty. By teaching only two courses that fall semester, I was able finally to write finis to "Quantitative Separation of the Halides and Halates in a Mixture of the Same." In November I went back to the university to defend my thesis. The following February, while I was buried in preparing the examinations for my own classes, the diploma came.

Mother Regina smiled broadly as I presented it to her.

"Don't say it, Mother," I laughed, and repeated with her, "The obedient soul shall speak of victory."

Chapter Eight

In my years at St. Albert's we had endured the poverty of Bethlehem and Nazareth. At Padua we experienced not so much the poverty of the body as that of the spirit. This was our public life. We had bidden farewell to Nazareth.

Padua College in Tannerton is by no means pretentious, as colleges go. It has no swimming pool or riding stables or miles of rolling, wooded campus. Walking down the sidewalk of Motling Street, you are at its entrance almost before you are aware of it. And riding up Coxwil Avenue, you might pass it right by, its façade half-hidden as it is by two venerable silver poplars. But if you are traveling in spirit (which is the most magical of all means of transportation), you would be drawn to it sweetly and unerringly. Its wonderful intangibles act like magnets. These intangibles of Padua are bound up with the great fivefold Franciscan ideals that form the preamble of its philosophy of education.

From the day Padua first emerged as a senior college, its faculty has been true to the ardent desire of its founder and first president, Mother Mary Regina. Concluding her first *Report of the President,* Mother Regina wrote:

> I pray that future years will always find a college staff zealously eager to inculcate in the minds of their students the great Franciscan ideals: that knowledge may never be divorced from personal holiness; that the universe may, indeed, be sacramentalized whereby all creation will lead to the Creator; that happiness does not lie in material goods; that simplicity is the daughter of truth; that the great Franciscan heritage of joy can be everyone's who will have Christ as the center of all being. May our College remain always Franciscan.

Now I was to have a share in this radiant ideal. As a student Sister years ago, I had come to appreciate how fortunate we were to have our own community college in which to earn our first degree. During those days of mingling study with prayer, of coupling research with spiritual reading, class lectures with religious instructions and conferences, I glimpsed a little of that great idea: knowledge must never be divorced from personal holiness. Moreover, I saw those ideals lived daily in the religious faculty who were not only my teachers, but also my elder Sisters in the same religious community.

Joining this faculty was to be the most humbling and inspiring experience of my life. To see at close range the unassuming virtues of many of my former teachers and to discover admirable qualities in others I had not known—this gave a marvelous impetus to my heretofore rather slow spiritual development.

The ring, symbol of our espousals to Christ, was the reminder to walk the path He had walked. From the cross Christ was saying, "Sister Jeremy, behold thy Mother, thy Alma Mater, Padua. Cherish her. She gave you intellectual birth in your novitiate and as a young professed. Now follow her precepts, guard her ideals, lead others on the way to Me." In those very words by which Christ had given us His Immaculate Mother, He was reminding me of this, my Alma Mater.

From the first, my self-will continued to plague me. I *loved* teaching high school. I didn't *want* to teach college girls. What possible interest could nineteen-year-old young women have in science, especially chemistry? They were sure to be a staid, sophisticated lot, far different from the delightful, unpredictable high school boys and girls. "Thy will be done," I'd say, close my eyes and see the smiling face of Sister Olivia. In the silent moments before sleep, I would hear her call, as it were, "Sister Jeremy, why do you wish your life away?" She was right. How foolish I was to hanker for days gone by while undreamed-of opportunities lay before me now! Daily I resolved to live in the present—and for the future; daily I broke my resolutions a dozen times.

God in His goodness had made loving arrangements for my frailty and inexperience. Sister Basil was again my superior; and how encouraging it was to have Sister Ida as head of the college chemistry department! They quickly proved the same invaluable guides and counselors they had been in those first rocky years at St. Albert's. Sister Cecile, too, was a familiar face; from St. Albert's she had been transferred to the college music department. The rest of the faculty were by no means strangers. Almost all had been my instructors and professors in my own college days. It was good to see Dr. Walters, head of the history department, still swinging his old battered briefcase down the corridor. His silvery gray hair was now a venerable white; he had already given almost twenty years of dedicated service to Padua. Even Jimmie, the "founding" janitor and brother of Mother Regina, was still hauling beds and blackboards around. On his carpenter's table each morning he picked up his day's agenda, S.O.S.'s from every department: "Jimmy, the shade in 303 is broken again." "Jimmie, please take the desk from 210 up to 409." "Jimmie, will you kindly varnish these two bookcases before Friday? Thank you."

But there was one person at the college whom I now was destined to know more intimately than ever before during student days: Sister Miriam, the dean of studies. In immediate charge of all scholastic life, of student schedules and the curriculum, she was always in demand by both students and instructors, never failing in serene and wise counsel. But what most endeared her to everyone was her enduring sense of humor which often took a philosophical twist. One hardly knew how to distinguish her wisdom from her wit. Her field was English; she held a Ph.D. from Catholic University. Beyond all this, she was a deeply spiritual Sister with an almost mystical insight. Few doubted that she lived in a high degree of union with God. But like all great people, she had her idiosyncracies—punctiliousness and fastidiousness.

Mother Regina had founded the college on sheer trust in God's loving Providence. The college was poor with the Faculty Patron, St. Francis of Assisi. The two chemistry laboratories, though equipped with superior apparatus, were pitifully cramped for space. Located at the west end of the ground floor of the scholastic building, they each measured eleven by thirty-six feet and housed a four-by-twenty-four-foot table. This allowed a total of three feet for both students and instructor to move about. Shades of St. Albert's community room! My vantage point would be at either of the doors to the corridor where, without a periscope, I would try to check technique and student apparatus.

One laboratory was heir to a bay with five windows. Here, nip and tuck, were placed two instructors' desks. And here, I sat ensconced behind my texts and workbooks one week before the opening of classes. Opposite, at the other desk, Sister Ida was busily typing her class notes. She stopped, noticing my dreamy stare toward the frosted windows. I saw neither mud nor stars. Sister Ida stopped typing. "Sister Jeremy," she advised, "watch your faith."

"Hmh?" I jerked my chin off the hand propping it. "Oh, I was just wondering how things are back at . . ." I stopped.

I *had* resolved to live in the present. But my hydra-headed self-will kept unwinding reels of imaginative films depicting the fun of high school teaching. Let Sister Ida extol the lovableness and charm of Padua girls—my fancy was laughing again at the antics of Red and Pete. Who wanted to teach science to girls who elected chemistry merely as a degree requirement? High school students not scientifically inclined avoided chemistry. A chemistry student is an enthusiastic sharpie, with nose keen for the rolling fumes of chemical reactions. College women! There was the rub! Imagine a sorority pledge tolerating stained hands. Fancy an aesthetic young lady appreciating the characteristic odor of each chemical.

"You'll get over it, Sister Jeremy. I felt the same way." Sister Ida, always the bright shaft to higher things, gently drew me back to reality. Her zeal had not waned; rather this new community assignment had accentuated her extraordinary enthusiasm for teaching—maybe, I thought, in complete resignation to God's Will. She guided me safely and surely through the maze of student semester hours, prerequisites, majors and minors, upper and lower division courses.

"Dear God, what a mess," I prayed.

My Guardian Angel worked hard. "Sister Jeremy," he counseled, "your community spent time and money to put you in this post. What about the trust it has placed in you for this work?" And, of

144

course, he was right. They were all right—God, Sister Ida, Sister Olivia and my Angel Guardian. I couldn't win—and I knew I really didn't want to. How had Sister Olivia put it? "We came to be religious, to obey . . ." So! Very well! I cut off all the heads of self-will "with one fell swoop." You win, dear Lord. You want me at the college, so here I am; and I'll try to like it! Thus I'd resolve again.

"That's the spirit!" Sister Ida saw the clouds lifting as I attacked the first day's lesson plan with something of my old zest. Yet many a prayer was mixed with thoughts, glazed windows, resignation, insufferable sorority women; but towering above them all serenely: "all the days of my life."

Preparing for classes and examining equipment took up all my time those few pre-school weeks, and I had not even walked around the buildings or campus since my return from the university. Accordingly, one afternoon I decided to tour. The college was constantly changing, stretching out into renovated rooms to afford further facilities. The library especially had long since outgrown itself at the rate of about ten books a day, necessitating the card catalogue in the corridor. I sauntered toward the library, noting the familiar bust of "dear old Will" on the card catalogue. There I found Sister Miriam.

"Why, Sister Jeremy! Did you come out of hibernation?" Sister turned to greet me, her large eyes expressing joyful surprise.

"Yes, Sister, I thought I'd better get the feel of the place before the big invasion Wednesday. Come to think of it, I might have known you would be here now."

"Yes? How so?"

It was more than I would have ventured to say to the dean Sister Miriam when I was a student. "We students had your number. Every day at this time you were to be found at the card catalogue or in the stacks."

"Really? It could not have been that bad."

"I suppose once in a while you were in the faculty library poring over trends and preparing to slay us with super college curricula."

"Sounds bad but I must be slipping. That was . . . how many years ago?"

"Right now it seems like a long, long time ago."

"Ah, yes, I remember." She smiled that wonderful smile of hers. "You were the class of novices that hoarded reserve books until you were caught."

"Yes, and then you gave us K.P., or should I say L.P. in the library."

"You remember that? We did get some extra work finished by taking advantage of your misdemeanors."

"Yes, and that was the only time I recall your letting us empty your waste basket."

"I suppose that is one of my peculiarities, Sister Jeremy: never let administration find you neglecting little homey duties. No woman should feel freed from daily time-consuming trivia. That is our heritage; as religious, the commonplace assume greater significance for eternity. So lived Mary, the mother of Christ."

"Sounds good. Like the old-time *assemblies of the Dean.*"

"Sister Jeremy, keep your sense of humor. I have a good joke for you during community recreation."

"I won't forget to remind you, Sister. Thank you so much." Sister Miriam stepped into the stacks.

Just like her, I pondered. *This* was the time for work; the joke was kept for *play.*

Except for such brief excursions, most of my energy and time were spent in the lecture room and chemistry laboratories. There were twenty-three in freshman chemistry. Seven juniors—"intruders"—were prospective high school mathematics and science teachers. This infiltration of juniors afforded competition for the freshmen. The juniors were saturated with education courses. They knew educational theories well—lesson preparation, presentation and recapitulation of subject matter. In the last row of lecture chairs they sat in judgment on my own teaching methods.

"Sister Jeremy, you do well for a beginning teacher," remarked Lorraine, a junior, after class one day.

"Thank you, Lorraine," I replied with inner amusement. "I hope to improve with practice." The next day Lorraine was very subdued. On inquiring, she had learned of my years of experience as a high school science teacher.

The freshmen who had taken chemistry in high school usually had all the answers. Their teachers had delivered chemical revelations to them—let no other Angel trumpet. And yet, they sometimes were utterly ignorant of basic chemistry. During class Lorraine ventured another condescending observation: "Sister Jeremy, I never did understand much of this in high school. You do simplify the theory. My high school chemistry teacher was not nearly so clear."

I would have none of this maligning of a defenseless high school teacher. "Lorraine, you must admit that this material is not entirely new to you. It takes time to assimilate theory. Also, in high school you neither studied so hard nor so consistently as now, nor did you have the mental maturity you now have presumably developed. That makes a difference."

Lorraine was not listening. "Oh, no, Sister Jeremy, that wasn't it at all. My chemistry teacher was so *brilliant* and knew so *much* chemistry that she just couldn't teach it!"

Rita, Lorraine's freshman sorority sister, added, "Yes, Sister, that's true. I had the same teacher myself. She had a master's degree, I think—maybe even a Ph.D. Do you have to have degrees to teach in college?"

Mother Regina surely had a good laugh over that one.

Sister Ida held department meetings on a fixed day every month. We discussed methods of teaching, new trends and developments, laboratory discipline and the dispensing of equipment and materials. "Sister Jeremy," Sister Ida advised at our October meeting, "you take too much for granted. Some, but not all, of your students have had high school chemistry. Many are weak in certain theoretical phases. Don't let their intellectual pose deter you from lecturing and demonstrating the basic principles."

Now I knew why my students' correlation of theory and experimentation was poor. Gradually I adjusted to the college pattern. And there emerged in my consciousness a truer picture of the college girl who elects chemistry. The science-minded young woman approached chemistry in the same manner as the serious high school boy. Many girls had acquired enough chemical vocabulary to impress their Notre Dame and Collegeville dates. There were a few aesthetic ones who became rapturously absorbed in the maze of flasks and test tubes of our boxcar basement laboratories. All this gave me confidence. Perhaps I was more successful than I realized.

But lest humility suffer unduly, episodes were never wanting to match my frustrating high school experiences. For instance, the lab manual directs the student to thrust a glowing splint into a bottle of oxygen to observe whether the splint is extinguished, continues to burn or bursts into flame. One day Rita came to me at my vantage point near the door. Holding a bottle of splints, "Sister Jeremy," she lamented, "I can't find the glowing splints. This is the only bottle of splints we have."

The study of iron corrosion is made by suspending clean iron nails in separate solutions of acids, caustics and other chemicals. The solutions are placed in test tubes. Then the nails are anchored at the head by a slipknot of string, the other end of which hangs over the side of the test tube. Thus, the nail can be pulled out of the solution at intervals and returned again while data are collected on the rate of corrosion in the various solutions. Poor Rita! She must have overlooked the word "nails" in the directions. I watched her pour out a neat little heap of pulverized iron and lower a loop of string around it. Carefully she tied a knot and lifted the string. Her face registered consternation when she saw but a few specks of metallic dust adhering to the string. I reached over and handed her the bottle with the iron nails. "Try this," I recommended. She sighed a thank you. Rita's boy friend was studying to be a chemical engineer at Collegeville. "Until death do them part . . ."

There were also novices in the chemistry classes. One of these, Sister Alberta, had been my chemistry student at St. Albert's. I noted with satisfaction how attentive she was to details. "Goodness, Sister Alberta," I remarked passing her place one day, "what a tremendous notebook you have!"

"Oh, yes, Sister," she rejoined enthusiastically, "these are the notes I've taken from Sister Ida's courses, and now I'm adding yours to them." She looked up bright-eyed. "I hope someday to be as good a teacher as Sister Ida." Then, with naïve simplicity, she added,

"You have some wonderful ideas too, Sister, and I'm jotting them down with Sister Ida's."

I smiled, remembering my own early dreams of being a science teacher. "Don't be too disappointed if your first assignment is not in the science field. Keep your Latin and German in good shape!"

She laughed, for the remark brought back memories of my ill-fated Latin and German classes at St. Albert's. From time to time Sister Ida, with Mother Regina's permission, allowed Sister Alberta to supervise the freshman chemistry laboratory. Her lesson plans were excellent, her supervision well directed, and her checking of students' laboratory experiments exact. She showed a healthy initiative too, as the day she casually asked in quantitative analysis class, "Sister, would you mind if I placed the guide along this side of my buret?" Immediately it occurred to me how much more practical her suggestion was than the usual placement. Sister Alberta's comprehension of theory and co-ordination of material improved with each additional course. In many ways her adeptness for chemistry pointed toward greater efficiency and practicality.

I suppose what I missed most during my first years in college teaching was what every Sister so fondly calls "mission life." We always contrasted "mission life" with "institutional living," and the latter generally came out on the short end. First of all, most of our missions are small parochial schools, and there are fewer Sisters. Relationships are bound to be closer and the Sisters' interests more tightly knit. There seems to be more interdependence: any event—a Christmas program, First Communion, graduation—calls for practically everyone's getting into the act. Then, mission living quarters, whether in a large or small house or apartment building made over into a convent, offer a homier atmosphere. When first coming to St. Albert's after six years in the mother house with its high ceilings and painted walls, I was struck by the homelike flowered wallpaper. Finally, the schedule makes a big difference. Classes on mission begin and end at the same time so that all the Sisters are usually together for the after-school recreation before prayer. But college classes are strung out from early morning until suppertime. The intervals between, not common to all, are usually devoted to preparing class lectures, checking assignments or correcting examinations. Besides, the institutional houses have two shifts for prayer and meals. Thus, with upward of forty-five Sisters on the college faculty, my chances of seeing and talking to each one every day were practically nil.

These contrasts continually reawakened my persistent self-will. I worked at it hard with prayer and the old theme song of obedience, but it was Sister Miriam who finally silenced the tempter.

"Sister Jeremy," she called as I was crossing the campus one afternoon late in October.

"Yes, Sister Miriam?" I waited for her at the "Holy Family" tree. Named for the tiny shrine of the Holy Family placed in a hollow of its trunk and covered over with glass, the giant cottonwood was a campus landmark.

"Beautiful day. Were you going for a walk?" She made it sound like a good idea. I decided the research I had planned could wait.

"Yes, let's!" It wasn't often the dean invited one for a leisurely round of the campus. The elms, tawny and breeze-blown, bowed gracefully to their sister maples, flamboyant in carmen red. Frisky squirrels played tag in the ankle-deep fallen leaves under the boxwood trees.

"What a world of yellow!" I ventured, as we stood in the lane lined with elms.

"Like Hopkins' own 'goldengrove,'" she rejoined.

"Do you know, Sister—" turning to her confidentially—"I really missed the campus when I went to St. Albert's. We didn't have much of a yard there."

"Yes, I know." She smiled at my surprise. "Why, I taught there myself, Sister Jeremy. But that was years before your time."

"Oh! I didn't know that!"

"Yes, years and years ago."

We were turning south from the north wall. From this far point, one has a good view of both the mother house and college buildings, with the academy wing extending along the west. The convent bell in the little steeple was catching the last shafts of sunlight. Except for the distant rumble of the highway, no sound disturbed the tranquil scene until I blurted, "Sister Miriam, did you . . ."

"I know what you're going to ask. Believe me, Sister Jeremy, you'll get used to the college. There are advantages, you know." Sister paused, teasingly, as though she sensed my *dare you to mention one.* Quickly she took up my unvoiced challenge. "Just look at this beautiful campus and recall St. Albert's tiny patch of grass."

"Think of the cultural opportunities," she continued, "the assembly speakers, the fine arts and dramatic programs, the special observances, exhibits, that punctuate the round of college days."

Of all that she mentioned, my greatest interest centered in our visiting lecturers. The outstanding ones in my mind are Fulton Sheen, Aline Kilmer, Richard Pattee, Arnold Lunn, Frank Sheed, Maisie Ward, Otto Eisenschiml, Catherine de Hueck, Eddie Doherty, Mortimer Adler, Carlos Romulo.

"You remember all these, Sister Jeremy? However, let's keep in mind what we share with all the mission Sisters: *this* is God's will for us. After all," Sister Miriam was adding by way of anticlimax, "*somebody* has to be at the college." Then we both laughed.

The bell in the convent steeple called us to Vespers. As I prayed it finally came home to me how foolish it is not to accept each assignment with gratitude, even with joy. I tried to make more room in my soul for that prime Franciscan principle: true joy can be the possession of those who will hold Christ as the center of their lives.

Soon I found the analytical chemistry class was really my pride and joy. These young women were chemical gluttons. They spent interminable hours in the laboratory. They pondered over schematic methods of separating the most difficult chemicals and then balanced the equations. I began to appreciate the woman in chemistry. Students like these were the scientists of the future. They would prove invaluable in medical fields and industrial control laboratories. Some would become theoretical chemists, working more with pencil and paper than in the laboratories. Others, who would master the technique of harmonizing theoretical and practical in a splendid pattern, would work as chemists. Could I have penetrated the future then I would have seen Paduan chemistry majors in all of these fields and more besides.

As semesters rolled by, I found myself becoming more and more a part of the college. It was, as I said, a most inspiring and humbling experience. What seemed to crystallize the impression most was the monthly faculty meeting. I felt not unlike Alice in Wonderland when all around me I heard learned reports and discussions of complicated educational problems.

During my third year at the college, Sister Ida retired because of failing health. But she remained in residence and continued to be my moral support. Sister Miriam made arrangements to relieve the burden of the department, which now rested on me. She scheduled two laboratory classes parallel. While this did not lessen my supervising duties, it did release me from the laboratory four to eight hours a week. She also recommended that Mother Regina engage the aid of an industrial chemist to lecture the three-hour-a-week course in physical chemistry. The newcomer to the department proved to be none other than Dr. Britt of university days, now a research chemist. This was a distinct advantage. He knew what industry expects from the bachelor of science and could brief the students on many practical aspects.

I myself kept abreast of fast-changing trends in the field by attending meetings, national and regional, of the American Chemical Society, the American Association for the Advancement of Science, and Sigma Xi, the national scientific honor society. Within a few years Padua banded together with a group of Tannerton industrial chemists and the chemistry faculty of Tannerton Junior College to form a local section of the American Chemical Society. From its origin Padua has been host to the monthly meetings.

Another development was the arrangement agreed on with nearby St. Charles Hospital to register its student nurses for courses in microbiology, dietetics, sociology, ethics, anatomy and chemistry. Their tightly packed hospital schedule necessitated our telescoping the courses in general, organic and biological chemistry into one semester of four hours a week. Correlating material for these accelerated lectures required intense preparation. Pedagogically the program was unsound, but for the time being little else could be done.

I missed Sister Ida more and more. Yet she had not abandoned me entirely. Indeed, she had more time now to observe the department undistracted by the rapid pace of a daily teaching routine. Our meetings consisted of what Sister Ida called "luxuriating in long-range planning," allowing us to discuss our mutual dream of a new science building and immediate improvement, such as reorganizing laboratory regulations. We introduced the honor system by which the students had free access to the store room and punched their own breakage cards. After several discussions of this sort, Sister Ida one day suggested that we meet with the dean. I was reluctant. "But why, Sister Ida?" I protested.

"I think you have some excellent ideas, Sister Jeremy, and I want Sister Miriam to talk them over with us."

The following day at three, Sister Ida and I sat before Sister Miriam in her inner office.

"Now, Sister Jeremy," Sister Miriam eased the slight tension at once, "what are these ideas that Sister Ida thinks are so wonderful?"

"Well . . ." I began tentatively, but the kindness in her eyes gave me the needed confidence. "I am thinking of the curriculum in the science department. We have a History of Physics course, a History of Biology course and a History of Chemistry course. Since the early history of all three fields is so similar and so interdependent, I thought we might substitute one History of Science course for these three. It would be an integrating factor. Besides, as matters stand, there are so few students registered in these courses that the respective course is now offered in alternate years. One inclusive history course could be taught every year by one instructor instead of three."

Sister Miriam listened with thoughtful interest. She was silent for a moment when I had finished and then spoke in that soft but decisive tone of hers. "Sister Jeremy, that's a splendid idea!" But she had a way of immediately rebounding from the ideal to the practical. "There's just this little detail: who would teach such an integrated course?"

Presumption or generosity? I considered neither. "I . . . I think I would like to, Sister."

Sister Miriam remarked with a smile, "You're real game, Sister Jeremy."

But Sister Ida was dealing out cold sober facts, "That course will take a tremendous amount of preparation."

Only then did I realize for what I had blindly bargained. "I suppose it will be another proof of 'Fools rushing in . . .' "

Sister Miriam laughed, "Well, since the 'angels' fear to tread anyhow, it looks as though the job is yours, Sister Jeremy."

I thought of Sister Benign, Sister Cosmas and Sister Florian, with their large classes in botany, microbiology, genetics, histology and anatomy; of Sister Rose Clare in physics, her ill health already necessitating a lighter schedule. To me it seemed the courses would benefit students and instructors as well. I was young (as nuns go) and in good health. I felt that with God's help I could do it: "I'm willing to try," I offered aloud.

"That's splendid! Now," Sister Miriam went on, "what about those other ideas? You might as well go all the way."

"Sister, the next one has to do with the increasing demand for women in the fields of scientific editing and librarianship."

"Yes, Sister Jeremy." Then with a mock patronizing air she asked, "What would you propose?"

"Oh, nothing revolutionary. Just that the girls be alerted to these fields and that those who like writing realize the advantage of combining science with editing or library research."

"I'm working on the new folder for the department, Sister," put in Sister Ida. "I can make a point of it there. The English and library science teachers could give us a little commercial in class, I'm sure."

"Fine. What else?" encouraged Sister Miriam.

"A new course for the chemistry or science major," Sister Ida announced. "Sister Jeremy had in mind a course in scientific literature and reference. We've been talking it over and I've already started to outline the subject matter. Knowing how jealously you guard the liberal arts ideal, we thought we could take care of it in a one-hour course."

"Yes," agreed Sister Miriam, "by no means do we want courses to pile up that result in a narrow specialization without a liberal arts background."

"Thank you very much, Sister Miriam and Sister Ida."

With heightened enthusiasm, I left the office.

As if to confirm this interview, Corn Products phoned for a chemical librarian.

Tannerton industries were clamoring for women chemists in control laboratories, for women as chemical editors and secretaries. This even awakened the resident students to similar opportunities in their own cities. So great was the influx the following semester that we formed three divisions of freshman chemistry. Dr. Britt was kind enough to teach another class.

To reduce the wear and tear of laboratory supervision, I often demonstrated experiments, especially in the early part of the semester. In the case of the reduction of copper oxide to pure copper by means of hydrogen gas, I pointed out the danger of the experiment.

"Girls, one must be very careful with hydrogen in the presence of a flame. It could blow the roof off this place."

Then I struck a match to light the burner in order to heat the oxide. Instantly there was a slamming of books, a shuffle and a swish. I looked up to see a girl dashing from her place in the last row and out the door. Other students turned around, puzzled. I was perplexed, too, but finished the experiment without incident.

After class I trudged to the community room. Between this room and Sister Basil's office were forty pigeon holes for our mail. I put my hand into an empty box and grunted, "Nothing, as usual. My brothers have given up the art of communication."

"Well, let's feel sorry for ourselves," plagued Sister Elsa, assistant dean of women, as she reaped a few pieces of advertising.

"Even John Wiley and Henry Holt failed me today," I lamented mildly.

"By the way, Sister Jeremy, what happened to June in class today? Did you know that she withdrew only an hour ago?" Sister Elsa was obviously troubled.

"She did?" I exclaimed in surprise. "No wonder she left class in such a hurry! But why did she bother to come at all if she was withdrawing?"

"Sister Jeremy, June is recovering from a nervous condition. You must have frightened her. She rushed up to her room, packed, called her mother and left. The dean said she phoned from the depot. If you keep on, we won't have any students by Christmas."

When Sister Ida heard of this she jokingly considered posting a sign in the chem lab:

ENTER

Only women with Fe constitutions

"Sisters!" was Sister Basil's warning voice, as she stood at the open door of her office. "What on earth is the matter? These are quiet hours for faculty and students. And what is more important, our religious rule intends recollection time to be spent on our assigned work."

Sister Elsa curtsied and left.

All my sails were down, but I was still my father's daughter. I was about to take exception when Sister Basil stole the march and ushered me into her office. The years made no difference. It was a reverent fear that I always experienced in her presence.

"Close the door, Sister, please," she directed. "Be seated, please, Sister Jeremy."

"Thank you, Sister Basil." With a fluctuating temperature I took the proffered chair.

"Sister Jeremy—" Sister Basil overlooked my discomfort—"do you remember Eugenia at St. Albert's?"

"Sure! Is that all you wanted?"

"Here is a card from her."

"Oh, you mean I really got mail?"

"Well, take it and read it."

DEAR SISTER JEREMY:

Greetings! Remember us?

Have been distressed by recent publication of stories concerning nuns who left their convents.

How about writing about nuns who persevered, and so put a better taste in our mouths?

Love and prayers from all of us—especially

EUGENIA AND FRED

"Eugenia wrote that. Fred never would write."

"I don't care which of the two wrote it. I am more concerned with their request."

"Who can do something about it? I teach science. I am not an English major. Even if I could and time were available, it would take me forever."

"Sister Jeremy, any of our Sisters' experiences would no doubt be fascinating."

There was a light rap followed by the opening of the door. "Surprise! Mother Regina," we both said as we rose.

"Mother Regina, would you like to read the card Sister Jeremy received today?"

"Nothing serious, I judge."

During these moments, I was battling the pros and cons.

"Mother, do you mind if I venture into storyland?"

Handing me the card, Mother replied, "I have no objections, Sister Jeremy. You have my sanction and my blessing."

"Thank you, Mother. You know I can't write that overnight."

"Sister Jeremy," tuned in Sister Basil, "I'm glad to note the lilt in your voice."

"Wish me luck, Sister Basil. Maybe I'll get something done during Christmas vacation. Thank you again, Mother, I must be going now."

Five months later I still had only a blank paper. No, not exactly—

I had a mere outline of what I thought would make a story about nuns who stayed. I started to pray to St. Jude "of impossible cases." This would probably constitute the most perplexing petition to date.

That summer it was a relief to teach only one hour a day. I tried to cull flowers of recollection from the Sisters. They were overwhelmingly co-operative. But I frequently preferred the indirect approach. Joining an evening recreation group, I would tune in for the amusing and interesting reminiscenses that rippled out from all sides. Many did not know of this project. I felt like a spy attending a secret meeting in disguise.

Meanwhile, I wondered about the beginning of school. The increased enrollment and the fact that Sister Ida had had no actual replacement disheartened me. Were Reverend Mother and the council aware of the acute situation in the chemistry department? I prayed the Stations of the Cross nine times daily that God would send help through the intercession of the Poor Souls. At least Sister Olivia ought to come to my assistance.

Sister Alberta had made final profession that summer. I was extending sympathy to her on the death of her mother. "Thank you, Sister Jeremy," she said gratefully. Then she leaned over confidentially. "I don't want to be inquisitive, but you must want something very badly the way you are saying Stations every day."

"Yes, Sister Alberta, I'm desperate." I bared my troubles, for I knew Sister Alberta had a warm spot for the chemistry department.

"Don't worry, Sister," she comforted. "My mother gives me anything I want. I'll pray to her for you. Help will come."

"God bless your dear heart."

A week later we sat in the auditorium to hear the year's appointments. I waited tense, hoping Mother Regina would include another chemistry teacher on the Padua list. Not one Sister was called with the proper qualifications. Baffled, I had a vague recollection of hearing Sister Alberta's name read.

At breakfast recreation the next morning, Sister Alberta came over to me. "Sister Jeremy, I'm going to be *here*—just think of it!" She was all youthful eagerness.

"Yes, Sister, welcome to the college staff." I answered blankly. "As a math major, you'll be an asset to that department."

Sister Alberta's blue eyes widened. "Sister Jeremy, you mean you don't know? Mother Regina told me I'm to help *you!*"

"Me?" I blurted with tears of unbelief and delight.

Sister Alberta appreciated my reaction. "What a jolt! You know I have only six courses in chemistry. How can I be of much help? See what my mother did to me to help you!"

No one appreciated this twist of heavenly humor more than I. "Sister Alberta, you are part of my hundredfold!" And I gave her a big hug.

Chapter Nine

No one except a member of the faculty of a small private college can comprehend the full meaning of one word in our language, the word *extracurricular*. Oh, yes, I thought I knew the meaning of *extracurricular*—"outside the running course." The difficulty lay in determining what comprised the "running course"—though I had no trouble understanding why it was called "running."

My initiation into this interesting aspect of college faculty life took place on "Invasion Day," formally known as student arrival day. One week before, I had come into the community room to find a number of my illustrious confreres (consoeurs?) studying the bulletin board intently. The semitransparent wall of Sisters' veils had often tempted me to succumb to a bad habit of ignoring bulletin notices, trusting that "tradition" would eventually be informant. But I had also lived long enough in the convent to know that some notices carry assignments which only the persons concerned take time to read. Reluctantly I attached myself to the fringe of the pulsating group of Sisters, hoping someone would clear a space before the bell called us to prayer. Finally Sister Ida saw me and from her vantage point, read my appointment: "Sister Jeremy: run the elevator."

"All year?" I asked in surprise.

"No, silly!" She laughed. "Just on the day the students arrive. The new students are too excited to learn even the simplest button system, and the old-timers are so loaded down with baggage they can't find a finger free to push the button. You'll find out. Sister Amy is to relieve you."

"Running the elevator is easy," I quipped in the bliss of my ignorance. Happily I did not understand Sister Ida's look, or I would have spent days of painful anticipation, besides the hours of actual weariness and sheer physical fatigue. The experience was calculated to retard or accelerate my sanctification—it was up to me.

At 7:30 A.M. on that particular "Day" of my college life, I fortified myself with what I thought was a very substantial breakfast and took my post at the elevator—just in time for my first passenger. That is, I presumed that underneath the suitcases, briefcases, hatboxes, garment bags, blanket and tennis racket there would eventually emerge a teen-aged human female. So I let "it" en masse into the elevator. To my query of "Floor, please?" there came a muffled "Fourth," and we were on our way.

That was the beginning. All day long by the hour, increasing numbers of incoming students accompanied by papas, mamas, sisters, brothers and even an occasional grandma or grandpa, along with accessories, were loaded and unloaded at various floors. Papa wondered if he was getting his hard-earned money's worth, and mama was mentally measuring the closets for adequacy, feeling the mattress or inquiring anxiously about the food. Now and then Sis had a hard time convincing her little brother that he should put down the stuffed tiger cub he was carrying; not a few embarrassed mamas chided tomboy little sister for calling her brothers from one end of the hall, "just to hear the swell echo."

By ten-thirty I started to feel inner hints that my substantial breakfast was wearing off. Where was Sister Amy? Whenever the elevator stopped at the cafeteria floor, a stimulating aroma redolent of fresh coffee enticed me. I was yearning to get away from my boxseat at this series of real-life dramas. Boxseat? I had been standing for three hours! Still no Sister Amy! I supposed she had been detained by "extracurricular" duties herself. I offered up the privation of Mocha for the success of the scholastic year and made one more trip to fourth when along came Sister Amy. Breathless, she informed me that she had been detained by the "sir echoes" which were getting out of bounds.

Another little phase in my extracurricular education involved a turn at "Operation Lock-up." Every night a student, appointed by student government, and a faculty member checked all outside doors and all windows on the first floor. This was a thirty-minute procedure. It also included making sure that the irons and faucets had been turned off in the girls' laundry and that all the lights, except the night lights, were extinguished. On such a round of duty I waited for my companion, one of our Chinese students, at the trysting place, the main entrance, on the first floor. Fifteen minutes passed. No Chi Peng. Up to her room I trudged. A muted "Yes?" answered my knock. I opened the door, and there stood Chi in her beautiful Oriental kimono, looking sadly perplexed.

"Chi, did you know this is your night to help check the building?"

"Seester, no go," remonstrated Chi, looking sadder.

"Yes, I can see that," I retorted as sweetly as I could manage. "But come now, Chi. It's getting late. You want to take your turn like the other girls, don't you?"

"No, Seester, I no go from room," was the persistent rejoinder.

"But why, Chi? What's wrong?"

Chi pointed ominously beyond my shoulder. "Dead Seesters out there," she announced solemnly.

I smiled and shook my head. "No dead Sisters are out there, Chi. Where did you ever get that idea?"

"Thee girls tell me, say dead Seesters' spirits walk in corridor after dark."

Those girls, I thought to myself, forever putting ideas into the foreign students' heads! This was worth a good laugh!

"Chi," I began to explain patiently, "you know we wouldn't hurt you while we're alive. Surely we wouldn't harm you after we're dead. Besides," I argued, "the other girls go into the corridors after dark, and no spirit bothers them."

But Chi was ready. "Seester, girls Christian; me pagan. Seester spirits not hurt Christians, but hurt pagans . . . maybe." The slight rising inflection revealed uncertainty, and working on that, I finally persuaded her to try just once. To her great relief, of course, we met no dead Sisters' spirits; none materialized—if one may use that term.

On the academic side, my appointment as moderator of the

Baconian Club, the college science organ, afforded a variety of interesting and liberalizing extracurricular activities. With memories of Jack and "The Lion Tamer," I wondered how I would fare with a college girls' club. At our first meeting, I encountered exactly four members: Pat, Sue, Agnes and Mrs. Miller. Pat, a bright-eyed Irish girl from Chicago, was a hard worker with ambitions in the medical field. Sue, on the other hand, came from a town downstate. With her champion collection of freckles (which she called her "specklations") and her amusing drawl, she was an easy but good-natured target for teasing. Agnes had come to us from Formosa through the National Federation of Catholic Students Overseas Project. She had been in the ranks against the Reds and had lost her father and a brother. Her gauntness added inches to her unusual height, yet she bristled with energy to defend her country and her faith. Mrs. Miller, a small efficient young woman and a registered technician, commuted from Ottawa. She had seen service and was availing herself of the G.I. Bill of Rights to complete her studies for a Bachelor of Science degree.

St. Albert's experience had taught me that stimulating activities would swell the membership. Our club accordingly requested an all-college assembly and drew up a program: "The Autobiography of the Soybean." The characters, Hoy Soy, Loy Soy and Joy Soy, dressed in homemade Chinese costumes. The assembly, pronounced most enjoyable by the student body, achieved results. Other science students joined the Baconian Club. This meant planning a variety of meeting programs and field trips to keep the club thriving and profitable.

Although we visited such imposing places as the Argonne Laboratories and the Museum of Science and Industry in Chicago, it was our field trip to Ottawa and Starved Rock that crept most often into the girls' reminiscences.

On that occasion the November wind was cold, misty and threatening. Sister Oliver, dean of women, thought we should stay at home. However, feeling that the life of the Baconian Club was at stake, I fearlessly decided, "We'll battle the elements." Jogging along in a chilly bus, we prayed the Rosary, Sue and Pat leading;

we chatted, dozed or sang, as the spirit moved us. Before we reached the Ottawa Peletier Marble Factory, the sun fought its way through and scattered the dark clouds.

After directing our group on a tour of the factory, the personnel showered us with glass souvenirs—marbles, vigil-light holders, head and taillight glass and similar curiosities. Later in the month some of these specimens were used as gifts for the orphans' birthday party conducted by the Sodality. Other samples, used by freshmen for a "marble roll" in the second floor of Scotus Hall, provoked the ire of the dean of women. One cannot foresee everything!

By way of detour on this field trip and before continuing on our way to Starved Rock, we stopped at the home of Mrs. Miller, who insisted on our visiting her home in Ottawa. The girls unpacked the lunch prepared that morning in the home economics laboratory. Though not a Catholic, Mrs. Miller expressed her appreciation of Padua's scholastic reputation and friendly spirit.

"In my youth I had been taught," she repeated that morning for the benefit of the girls, "that Heaven was just a place where one didn't work. I like work. I was not interested in that kind of Heaven. But Padua has made me aware of the immense activity and the true ways of God." She acknowledged the religious spirit, deep but unobtrusive, that pervaded the entire campus, and the delightfulness of student activities so impressed her Protestant family that she influenced them to lose a life-long prejudice.

After enjoying Mrs. Miller's hospitality we sang the blessing of St. Francis: "May the Lord bless thee, may the Lord keep thee . . ." Our bus transported us to our final destination, Starved Rock.

The unique beauty and historical interest of this landmark were not lost on the girls. Its story reiterated the ever-present tragedy of man fighting fellow man in a setting of natural beauty which God certainly never intended for man's hate.

About this time UNESCO made headlines. Baconians voted it the theme for a radio program. WTAN, the local Tannerton station, released a half hour every Tuesday evening to the Padua Radio Workshop. Though the Speech Department was in general charge, various departments often arranged musical, dramatic or educational programs. To give our science broadcast popular appeal, I asked Agnes to present a brief statement of what UNESCO meant to Formosa.

As a child I had lived in a cosmopolitan environment. I thought I understood nationality traits fairly well. My schoolmates had been Swedes—diligent, slow, deliberate, consistent; French—delightful, precise, enthusiastic; Poles—hotheaded, imaginative, loyal; Germans—determined, steady, ambitious; Irish—playful, witty, kind; Bohemians—quick, methodical, clever. Yet in my ignorance, I sallied forth.

"Agnes," I said, meeting her in the chemistry corridor. "Would you like to be on our radio broadcast?"

"Do not have the time, Seester," she answered, shifting her book load to the other arm.

That sounded final. But a few days later as I sat at my desk timing the program and pondering over a substitute, a rap vibrated my door. The door swung open and in came Agnes. She began abruptly, "Seester Jeremy, what you want me do on radio? How much time I have?"

Neither honeyed words nor stern statements would convince Agnes that I could not possibly give her our full radio time. This episode took place exactly two weeks before the program. But daily, to Agnes' supreme annoyance, I would ask, "Is your speech ready? May I see a copy?" After ten days Agnes submitted a veritable ream of material. "That's fine, Agnes," I told her. "I'll check and cut it to the allotted ten minutes."

Agnes' bright almond eyes opened wider. "No, no!" she blurted excitedly. "You not know to cut!"

Back went the ream to Agnes. Three days before the broadcast I called her and said, "Agnes, we have a practice tomorrow night at seven in the radio studio. Be there."

"I not sure. I see. If not too busy, I come."

The next morning Agnes greeted me, all anxiety and frustration. "Seester Jeremy, why they not tell me? How I know they have the semifinals? Now I study for examinations. I cannot be on broadcast."

Beyond the argument and persuasion stage, I sighed, "All right, Agnes. I'll ask Father Kenneth to do your part."

Father Kenneth, a tall jovial Franciscan in the religion and philosophy department, had once been a missionary in China. Father graciously promised, with these words, "If you need me, Sister, I'll be there."

"But, Father," I implored, hoping for something more definite, "Agnes has already told me she wouldn't do it."

Father grinned in a "Hold on and you'll see" sort of way, and left me still with a very dubious ten minutes to be accounted for. Studio-bound a half hour before going on the air, a swarm of students and faculty greeted me with "Sister Jeremy, Agnes is looking all over for you."

Then Agnes caught up with me. "Time we go on air?" she casually asked.

With an effort to sound just as casual, I replied, "Seven-thirty, but the studio doors will close to all but the cast at seven-fifteen. Let me see your script." I scanned the pages of tiny broken lettering she handed me. "This is excellent, Agnes, but still too long. You'll have to cut it." Now we were in the studio.

The countdown started. We were on the air. Waiting her cue, Agnes sat with pencil—marking, reading, reading, marking. In the middle of someone's script, she groaned in a whisper, "Cannot cut! Cannot!" The next minute she was on the air. Her timing was perfect. WTAN's most favorable comments were for Agnes. Most important to her, she had not "lost face."

With Baconian enterprises smoothly launched, I was honestly learning to like extracurriculars, when suddenly a new assignment landed right in the lap of my complacency. There it was on the neat pink slip in my mailbox in early September of my second year at Padua:

SISTER JEREMY:
Supervise Dorm 322. Occupy dorm cell. God bless you—and them!
                                    SISTER MIRIAM

What sort of tongue-in-cheek humor was this? I wondered if the conventual term "cell" didn't take on added meaning in a case like this. Oh, well, let's go see what God's Will had in store in 322.

In residence quarters at Padua there are three large dormitories, each housing ten girls. Five double-deck beds line the inner walls. Along the four windows is adequate space for dressers, desks and book racks. The dorm mother's cell is a little room off the short hall leading from the dorm to the bathroom, directly opposite the large closet. I entered 322 as the "mates" were getting settled on arrival day. They looked up with friendly smiles from the silks and notions of their unpacking, as I announced, "I'm Sister Jeremy, your neighbor," and gestured toward my cell. At once they surmised our relationship and welcomed me to their circle with a spontaneous warmth that was as sincere as it was charming. Introductions tumbled out. "I'm Nancy. This is Dolores—or is it Rose?" And the volunteer emcee giggled. "No, I'm Rose," corrected another voice, "and that's Dolores there. What did you say your name is?"

"Janet."

"And you're Julia—from Ohio, right?"

"Yes, that's right. From St. Albert's in Ohio."

I leaned around bobbing heads to get a better look at Julia. It was years since I'd been at St. Albert's; I couldn't have taught her, but perhaps I had had her older brother or sister.

She came closer and answered my unasked question. "Sister Jeremy, I've heard about you. Remember my sister, Eugenia?"

"Eugenia!" I exclaimed. "You do resemble her! I knew I had seen you somewhere before!" She smiled with girlish pleasure. "Let me see," I went on, "you were in the grades then. Tell me: how is Eugenia, and how is your sister Dorothy?"

"They're both fine, Sister. Eugenia is expecting in January, you know."

"Oh, that's wonderful! And what about Dorothy?"

She laughed. "Well, she's practically engaged."

The chatter continued above the clink of lotion bottles, the rustle of tissue wrappings, the snapping of suitcases, the opening and closing of drawers.

Julia deftly folded her lingerie, promising, "When I get unpacked, I'll tell you all about St. Albert's, Sister."

"I'd like that, Julia."

So we were acquainted, the seeds of friendship planted.

Supervision of a dorm also included rotating duty in Scotus Hall one night a week. This was a combination of reception and curfew committee-of-one. Ordinarily Wednesday, Friday and Saturday were date nights, the schedule on the desk indicating who was to come for whom and what time they were to return.

After this one-night-a-week stint till 1:00 A.M., the humble dorm cell was luxury. The manner of spending other nights as dorm mother was regulated by my degree of insomnia or ability to turn a deaf ear. Monday nights usually promised early retiring. Week-end activity and new scholastic assignments generally had soporific effects on the dormitory occupants. Tuesday to Thursday were variable. On these nights I prepared myself for any one of a variety of tasks and waited for atmosphere from "hit parade," friendly argument, incessant giggling over practical jokes, "the low-down" on faculty members, to ukelele strumming.

Being a dorm mother required different personality adaptations from being a teacher of chemistry. In science one deals with facts, involving no emotional difficulties in making decisions. Laboratory formalities are standard; even variables follow a set curve. In everyday living right is still right and wrong, wrong. Decisions must be weighed but there are always individual, social and emotional differences.

The ease and rapidity with which the "dorm girls" formed a family group astounded me. I prayed God not to let such harmony be disrupted by my bungling efforts. The best course was to live and let live, but the girls claimed "squatters' rights" to the "dorm mother." I had to participate willy-nilly.

The evening before the girls' departure for Christmas vacation, all the "dormies" and I sat around the Christmas crib in the dorm, singing carols and exchanging gifts.

Nancy's sudden tears were not understandable, until between sobs we caught, "Sister, kids! Just think! I might have missed all this—if—if I had chosen a private or a double! God is so good to me. I might never have had all of you for friends. I'd never have tonight's memory...."

The other girls perhaps were not so articulate, but the quiet atmosphere acknowledged they were shareholders. The years evinced enduring loyalty from these friendships.

Friday evenings were comparatively free of regulations. No "quiet hours" until ten-thirty! One particular Friday night Rose had been strumming her ukelele all evening, and, to judge by the responsive singing, the "dormies" were enjoying it. In my cell bunk I lay patiently enduring their legitimate pleasure. At ten-thirty the "dormies" were in no mood for quiet. No one was minding the clock. The ukelele was still plinking away. At ten-forty I rapped on my window adjoining their room. There was a lull; then, as though they did not trust their ears, a timid *"boing?"* like a musical question mark was wafted from the uke. I answered with a second and louder rap. A third would mean a demerit. The message got through. All was quiet.

But ukelele nerves demand retribution. Saturdays were "sleeping-in" mornings—provided the dorm was ready for inspection by ten-thirty and the "dormies" were willing to forfeit breakfast. At seven-thirty, having been up two hours and fortified with all my religious exercises, I climbed the stairs to the third floor. Every one of the ten was sound asleep. The green wound cried revenge. I couldn't resist. From bed to bed I strolled, strumming improvised melodies on Rose's uke. In five minutes the whole dorm was up!

Supervising a dormitory also enlarged my curriculum. Sometimes I was surprised at my own versatility: English, Latin, mathematics, German, history, religion, crocheting, knitting, darning, counseling, strumming. The paradox was counterplot to my reputation. For instance, one day Jan came back from class with the remark, "Sister Jeremy, we made a mistake in that translation last night." On another Julia said mischievously, "Sister, guess what I got on our theme—C. But Sister Jarlath liked our title." Hints about this convenience had been dropped to neighbor "privates" and "doubles." Chemistry students took advantage of the closeness of my living quarters. By reason of Sister Ida's emphatic training, all laboratory notebooks were due by midnight on the day of the experiment. The scholastic building was locked at nine in the evening. Occasionally, at eleven fifty-five, in my drowsy state, what I might have mistaken for a rodent visitor was only a chemistry student slipping a notebook under my door. Oh, the joys of a campus "dorm prefect" were unparalleled, unless surpassed by those of an off-campus house mother.

Padua had three such houses for upperclassmen, located about two blocks east of Scotus Hall on Ridge Street. I was assigned to Bonaventure Hall the year that Pat and Sue resided there as seniors. Here, once in a while, selfishness shadowed the family spirit so prevalent in the dormitories. We had a pair of fudge makers who hoarded their product for nibbling in their rooms during quiet hours without fear of intruders. Their noses, however, always lifted to detect the aroma of others' fudge in the making. Self-invited, they would appear in the snack room for the testing. Foreseeing this on one occasion, I decided to be the seat of justice. Shortly before quiet hours, the two poachers directed their steps toward the kitchen whence wafted the aroma of delicious chocolate fudge. Instantly I swept into the kitchen and demanded, "What are you people doing here? Don't you know it's time to be in your rooms?" (It really was a minute early.) Sue, the culinary artist, was pouring her last pan of fudge. I was certain she realized I did not mean her. But in her excitement Sue handed the poachers the pan of fudge, and out they scampered.

"Sue," I asked in surprise, "what made you do that? I was trying to help you."

"You were, Sister Jeremy," fretted Sue in her inimitable drawl, "but I was so stunned to see you pop in like that, that I didn't stop to cut them a piece."

I went into my room and hung a placard for myself: Mind Your Own Business.

Another evening Sue had cut dinner hour to complete an experiment. On our way to Bonaventure, she said she'd like to stop at Van's snack shop on the corner. "Certainly, Sue," I agreed. "You run in. I'll wait." By this time every student was to be either in the library or in her respective place of study. I noticed Sue's embarrassment when we arrived at Van's. Looking in, my eye met Pat's. There she was, having a tête-à-tête with a boy friend. Her Irish face deepened in a fiery blush, and without so much as an "Ah, yes," or "No" to her bewildered companion, she fairly flew out of Van's, past me and down the street toward Bonaventure. By the time Sue and I got there, Pat was poring over the books. Her subsequent demerit, served by student government, brought chagrin of course, but her companions used the incident as fresh ammunition for teasing. "The night Pat broke the world's track record" they called it.

The Tannerton police cruisers are the personification of politeness and chivalry, especially if a Sister is the "damsel in distress." One evening I had just left Scotus Hall for Bonaventure, when a police car stopped and an officer called cheerily, "Sister, let us take you home." I had spent almost eight hours in the laboratory and was happy to accept. No sooner had I seated myself than they turned on the spotlight and siren, laughing at my protests. They didn't stop either, until they reached the driveway of Bonaventure Hall. Every girl's head appeared at the window to see whom the police had "picked up." Every head disappeared just as quickly when I stepped out of the car.

The next year I was transferred from Bonaventure to the neighboring hall, called by everyone in Tannerton, "The Castle." It was a palatial stone mansion patterned after European castles, with a terraced garden rising up from Valley Street. Once thriving with a variety of plants, flowers and shrubs, the garden had been somewhat neglected, but lilacs, peonies and roses still bloomed luxuriantly. Residence at "The Castle" was reserved as a senior privilege. Here the four-year friendships flowered as brilliantly as the outdoor beauties.

That same year there was excitement in Tannerton. The Archdiocesan Cardinal announced the creation of a new diocese, with Tannerton as its seat. We were to have our very own bishop! Everyone was overjoyed. Franciscan hospitality prompted Reverend Mother to offer our first bishop "The Castle" as a temporary residence. The offer being accepted, our family was separated. The girls were transferred to vacancies in the three remaining resident halls. No one ever knew what this break cost the girls. But they often reflected proudly, "We lived in the bishop's house."

"The Castle" was still our property. At graduation the bishop's grounds were a riot of peonies—the very flowers to decorate the altars. One early morning I loaded my arms with blooms. As I stood up to adjust my burden, I heard the sonorous voice of His Excellency, "So, Sister! Caught you red-handed this time—stealing my flowers!" I looked up to see him regarding me in evident amusement from the top of the back porch.

Chagrined, I asked, "What are you going to do to me, Bishop?"

"Well—" he grinned—"the least I can do is put you under interdict. That will keep you from the rest of the Sisters, so they don't learn bad habits. Of course—" he paused, with his Irish twinkle—"that also means you can't go to summer school."

I was walking toward him. "That's just fine, but would it prevent me from visiting your mother, Bishop?" I asked.

He beamed. "The dear soul would be delighted to see you, even under interdict. Come right in, Sister."

His mother was in her eighties, a smiling, silver-haired woman worthy indeed to have a son a bishop. She welcomed me warmly, admiring the peonies. I pleaded my cause.

"You know," the bishop defended, "these Sisters have me coming and going. When I was a little boy, they told me I should always obey my mother. Now they come and steal my flowers, then beg my mother to take their part. The only thing for me to do is let you go, Sister."

Soon after this, another distinguished prelate entered my life—Archbishop Mar Ivanios, the primate of Trivancore. His Excellency was soliciting aid for his colleges in India. He wanted very much to have at least two Sisters teach science in his women's college. We aided him with science curriculum outlines, bibliographies and apparatus lists. Perhaps some day this would mean my opportunity to be a missionary. Long-ago dreams floated in my fancy again, with the hope that maybe some day I could say, "America, I'm off for India!"

But college days rumbled on at Tannerton, keeping pace with a more mature and serious America, pushing forward in military and educational development. Time wrought its inevitable changes. Rita, Pat, Sue, Janet, Rose, Julia graduated and were replaced by other Pats and Sues. Always a St. Albert's girl graced Padua halls and kept me up to date. I heard with pleasure the news of a new grade school at dear old St. Albert's, and of plans for transferring the high school into the completely renovated old grade school building. The Sisters, too, at long last, were to move into a brand-new convent on the site of the old high school.

Then a great loss saddened us. Our beloved Mother Regina, after a painful illness that ennobled her great soul still more, departed from this life. Yet her spirit remained to inspire us, and the ideals she had first fired in the college torch flamed brightly through the years. We felt her unfailing solicitude from her place in eternity. At the general election our own Sister Elsa was chosen to succeed her. It was a distinct advantage to have our new Reverend Mother so conversant with college affairs, so cognizant of college problems.

Shortly after Mother Elsa's election, Sister Ida and I were poring over a revised curriculum in freshman chemistry when Mother stepped into the room.

"Sisters, I am so glad to find you both here."

"Yes, Mother. Is there something we can do for you?" was Sister Ida's ever ready offer.

"Let's be seated. I think this will take a while."

"Thank you, Mother."

"This is the problem. Here is a letter from the State Superintendent of Schools requesting us to offer a program in Civil Defense. The letter recommends that we apply to the National Laboratory and our local civil defense co-ordinator for a syllabus. Would you take care of this, Sister Ida?"

"Oh, yes, Mother. Sister Jeremy is always itching to do something more, something different and challenging."

"Come, now," I ventured. "It is not that bad."

"Not far from it," Mother turned to me smiling. "Thank you both so much. Keep me up to date with the program."

174

"We will do that, Mother," we both agreed, standing as Mother Elsa left.

"Well—now what?"

"I doubt whether it's as bad as it sounds," reassured Sister Ida. "I am glad that the Federal Government is becoming more and more aware of the ignorance and apathy of civilians concerning a possible radiological attack."

And so it was that the physics, chemistry, biology and natural science departments, with the aid of Argonne National Radiological Laboratory officials, prepared a course in civil defense. The enrollment of these classes reached the three-hundred mark, drawing teachers from over thirty parochial and public schools of the area.

But this was not the only occasion when Padua and Uncle Sam worked together.

At one of our departmental meetings Dr. Britt remarked, "Sister Jeremy, the arsenal is offering army surplus laboratory equipment at a nominal price to eligible schools."

"How do you go about getting it, Doctor?" I inquired.

"Apply to the State Superintendent of Schools. He will examine your educational status and decide whether or not you will be a beneficiary."

A few weeks later we received government application forms in sextuplet. After three months Sister Alberta, Dr. Britt and I were finally permitted to apply at the government laboratory. The arsenal was set back from the road so that the surrounding farmland deceived the passer-by as to its true location. We presented our credentials to three successive guards. The equipment stood where the last employee had left it. Beakers with reagents, flasks with unfinished reactions, apparatus setups—as though one had left for a coffee break. But in other places there was evidence that efforts had been made to protect delicate equipment by covering it carefully. Naturally on our tour we were supervised by an FBI agent. The equipment was labeled with government identifications, which had to be transcribed on six separate request forms.

Luckily, the distance was only twenty miles from Padua. It took a week's commuting to complete the inventory. We immediately realized that not only the chemistry department but the biology, physics, health education and natural science departments would also benefit from this rich reservoir filled with its excellent equipment.

Our frequent trips to the arsenal required the constant use of a car. Mother Elsa had bought a government surplus car for twenty-five dollars, "a penny a pound." Sister Alberta drove; I prayed. The car was a weak wash of regulation army olive green or whatever the pigment is called, the model of an ancient vintage. But it ran. . . .

One day Sister Alberta and I were returning after a trying ordeal of checking and rechecking. When we made the last turn in the road up the bluff leading to Padua, we noticed an army truck evidently stalled. Khaki-clad service men were sitting along the curb somewhat frustrated. As we drove up, they jumped to attention.

"What's the idea?" I said to Sister Alberta as we passed the receiving line.

"Didn't you see their faces?" she giggled. "Look back and you'll get the answer. I'm watching my side mirror."

I turned, and there, just coming around the bend was another army car, a newer, brighter model. I joined in her laughter. "Oh, for heaven's sake! They must have been expecting their officers with orders about the stalled truck. And who comes riding up in an army car but two creatures in medieval costume! No wonder they were dumbfounded!"

Finally our lists were sent to the State Superintendent of Schools. Two months later we received word that we might call for the material. Jimmie, our maintenance man, drove out in the convent truck, while Sister Alberta, Dr. Britt and I made the trip in the "penny a pound." After checking the numbers on the lists with the materials in the arsenal, under FBI supervision, we filled the truck. Thus do we live "all the days" in poverty. . . . A large outlay of money would have purchased this equipment quickly through one order list to a scientific apparatus company. Our hundredfold took days of labor and months of waiting, but like all good things hard come by, our Godsend was more thoroughly appreciated.

The new equipment emphasized still more sharply our ever present lack of space and outmoded accommodations. Well aware of our limited budget, I still thought something might be done. I appealed to Mother Elsa.

"Mother, you know our two eleven-by-thirty-six-foot laboratories can't hold the increasing influx of chemistry students," I told her one afternoon when she came to look at our cramped conditions.

"Yes, Sister Jeremy, I fully realize that," Mother sympathized. "With the universal growth of technology, more and more women are being attracted to the field of science. What would you say the percentage increase is?"

"I can't say exactly, Reverend Mother. But you can get a general idea if we list the fields of applied science which require a chemical background. Dietetics, bacteriology, medical technology, science editing, patent laws, medicine and science advertising are some of the positions which our chemistry alumnae are now filling.

"Making a rough estimate, I would say our enrollment has tripled in the last ten years."

"Sister Jeremy, I know something has to be done. We'll pray about it. St. Joseph will help, I'm sure."

"Just one more request, Mother, please?"

She smiled kindly, "Yes?"

"As you know, Dr. Britt, a consulting chemist, is directing our senior research students. Besides that, he is willing to take a division of freshman chemistry if we could find a place for their laboratory work. Our two laboratories take care of the upper division students, but they must always put away all their apparatus whenever freshmen are scheduled. We'd like the upper division classmen to use the laboratories at their available time."

Reverend Mother had been listening intently. Now she laughed a little and said, "Sister, I think you and Sister Alberta are autocrats in that, but it certainly is a wonderful advantage for the students."

"If only there were some place we could use," I lamented.

Mother Elsa sighed. "Sister Jeremy, you pray and give me time. Something will turn up. Right now, with all the additional needs of the community, the college will have to make the best of the present facilities."

It seemed like another case for St. Jude, and I feared the situation taxed even his miraculous resources. I prayed. But before the week was out, something *did* materialize. In fact, it had been there all the time! Across the street from the scholastic building was an old frame house owned by the convent; the top floor was used by two of our bachelor maintenance men as living quarters. "Why not," suggested Mother Elsa, "convert the first floor into a temporary laboratory?" In short order, the parlor, dining room and kitchen were each set up with a twelve-foot chemistry table. Here we moved the freshman classes, elegantly styling our new "space," St. Albert "Hall." We promised the good saint, patron of Catholic science students, that some way, some day we'd give him a "Hall" worthy to bear his name.

Mother Elsa stopped by the first day we initiated the freshmen.

"Look, Mother Elsa," I exclaimed happily, "now we can supervise twenty to thirty students at a time!"

"Will this ease the current crisis?" Mother asked.

"Yes, Mother, thank you! It was wonderful of you to think of this place. Now Sister Alberta, Dr. Britt and I can stagger our freshman laboratory periods, and our advanced students will have full use of the regular laboratories in the scholastic building."

This arrangement solved one problem, but another soon forced itself into the forefront of my consciousness. It dealt with Sister Alberta's further study. She had spent several summers at the university making up chemistry deficits, and by dint of hard work and sacrifice had taken the twelve-weeks courses from June to September for several summers to earn her master's degree in chemistry. But now I felt Sister should be given a sabbatical to round out her chemical knowledge, to enable her to concentrate on the field without the distractions of class preparation, laboratory supervision and checking of assignments.

Again I rapped at Mother Elsa's door. Mother's patience and graciousness edified me. Her life of constant interruptions in the midst of many heavy duties contrasted sharply with my impatience of students' problems.

"Mother Elsa," I began, "the chemistry department——"

"Sister Jeremy, I'm aware that you do need more room . . ." Mother said.

"Oh, that, of course, but this is something else. It concerns Sister Alberta. Don't you think it would be good to give her a sabbatical?"

Mother leaned forward. "A sabbatical? Now, Sister Jeremy, really! There is not a Sister we can spare to take her place, and Dr. Britt is doing all he can." She paused, and I breathed a quick message to St. Jude. "Sister Alberta is still young; probably in a few years we can see our way through." She rose and smiled encouragingly. "However, pray, Sister Jeremy, and if Heaven sends a solution sooner, so much the better."

"Thank you, Mother." I left her office with my brain churning. Heaven was stormed again. Of one thing I was certain, the inhabitants of Heaven were constantly reminded of Sister Jeremy and her problems—and took the lion's share in solving them. I had never doubted that Sister Olivia had not forgotten her old friend.

Gradually a plan shaped itself in my mind. "Sister Alberta," I said casually one Saturday morning. "I'm thinking of a way we could give you a sabbatical."

She squinted in mock suspicion. "Is it like the way I was brought into this department?"

"Well, yes, sorta." I laughed. "I did say a prayer to your mother."

"Go on, then, don't hold out on me. What's the latest weird idea you've cooked up?" she teased.

"Come with me to Sister Miriam and we'll see whether or not it's pedagogically safe."

Fortunately Sister Miriam was in her office. "Well," she began smiling, "how are things below deck?"

"Everything's fine, Captain," I laughed, "but we do have an idea we'd like to talk over with you. Don't you think Sister Alberta ought to have time out to do more graduate work in chemistry?"

"Of course, Sister Jeremy. That would be ideal," agreed the dean. "How would you like that, Sister Alberta?"

Sister Alberta was nodding rather incredulously, and I was thinking that perhaps Mother Elsa had already spoken to Sister Miriam. Instead she brought me up short with, "And how would it be done,

Sister Jeremy? Mother Elsa was just pointing out how desperately she is in need of Sisters, especially of science teachers. The whole nation is clamoring for science teachers, and you think we can spare an invaluable instructor? Have you mentioned this to Reverend Mother?"

"Yes, Sister," I answered rather forlornly, "but I wanted to check my plan with you." I paused. Sister Miriam was evidently waiting for my plan. I took the plunge. "You know, Sister, that Lorraine, who graduated six years ago and has her master's in chemistry, has been teaching at the junior college. I'm sure I could persuade her to take one of Sister's classes. Then there's Theresa—she's been science editor at Armour for five years—if she would take another class, we could possibly rotate courses for two years. This would not deprive any of our students of advanced courses and would give Sister Alberta two years and three summers for further study." I finished breathlessly and waited expectantly. Sister Alberta paled.

"Sister Jeremy," Sister Miriam said slowly, "it looks . . . wild to me now." I knew she reserved that word for only the boldest enterprises, but that it was in no way equated with the "impossible" in her mind. "Do you have this outlined?" she was asking.

"Yes, Sister, here it is." I handed her the typed sheet.

"You may leave it here with me. I'll discuss the plan with Mother Elsa. And," she concluded encouragingly, "if we think it will not tax you overmuch, we'll contact these alumnae and see what can be done." She smiled at Sister Alberta. "I would be the last one to deprive Sister Alberta of the opportunity to enrich her scientific background. I think you're doing wonders, Sisters."

The following summer Sister Alberta was relieved of her teaching duties to begin her work toward the doctorate.

The chemistry students were co-operative beyond my expectations. Best of all, Lorraine and Theresa were excellent instructors, and enjoyed being back at their alma mater. The monthly faculty meeting was an awakening to them.

"You know, Sister Jeremy," remarked Theresa after a lively discussion at one of the meetings, "I never realized how hard the faculty works for the good of the students. Why, this is tremendous!"

Lorraine joined us as we started over to Scotus Hall. "Sister, did you hear what Sister Miriam assigned me for the December meeting? A report on the trends in the teaching of science in the last five years, as stated in the *Journal of Higher Education*."

"You could do worse," Theresa told her. "My assignment for the January faculty meeting is to summarize the trends from the last ten years of NCEA meetings."

"That's great!" I put in. "You two are really getting a good initiation into college teaching. We've been doing such things for years."

We had reached the lobby entrance and paused before going our separate ways. "Too bad more of the alums can't come back and have our good fortune, Sister," said Lorraine. "I plan to tell everyone I meet what they're missing."

Their enthusiasm rekindled my own. I realized that I, too, had come a long way toward appreciating Padua. "Girls," I said, looking at my watch, "it's getting late—time for all weary college instructors to relax."

"That's right! Good evening, Sister!" they chorused. "See you tomorrow in the lab!"

Thus our "wild" plan became a reality. The students responded admirably to the alumnae teachers. From time to time they remarked about their efficiency, adding somewhat grimly, "And they can pile on the work too, just like the other faculty members."

Two years and three summers passed, and Sister Alberta was back. Her biochemical research was a beautiful piece of work. With all her examinations behind her, there remained only her thesis and its defense. That scholastic year Sister Alberta carried a representative teaching load.

In the spring of that first year of Sister Alberta's return we were taking inventory. I was juggling a handful of distilling flasks, while Sister Alberta entered specifications in our registry.

"What are you two up to?" We heard Sister Ida's voice above the clinking of glassware.

"Come in, and I dare you find an empty spot."

"Congratulations, Sister Jeremy. I thought you would be celebrating."

"Oh, that! I don't know if we will be able to go."

"Why, of course, you are going."

Sister Alberta, dismayed, was looking from one to another. "Going where?" she inquired perturbed.

"American Chemical Banquet," said Sister Ida at the same time as I said, "Las Vegas."

More confused than ever, Sister Alberta expostulated, "I don't follow at all. Do you know that you are talking different languages unless Las Vegas means American Chemical Society banquet?"

"We did say different words, didn't we?" Sister Ida looked shocked.

By this time I had scurried to the desk and procured that morning's letter.

"Read this, Sister Ida. My hands are soiled and I do not want to pull this out of the envelope. Read it aloud."

Sister Ida read:

Dear Sisters Jeremy and Alberta:
    You are hereby invited to attend a Test Shot at Las Vegas. This invitation is extended from the Federal Civil Defense Administration. Enclosed is a Staff Identification card that will be of assistance to you during your stay in Nevada. The date of the Test Shot will be sent later.
                         Yours sincerely,
                         [Signed] Civil Defense Executive

"Congratulations to both of you! But I have something better."

"Better? What could be better than that? You well know that these are desired pastures," said Sister Alberta.

"Sister Jeremy, please put those flasks on the shelves and be seated."

"Is it that bad?" I questioned, putting the dusty flasks on the shelf and wiping my soiled hands on the laboratory apron.

"Here is a letter Mother Elsa asked me to deliver. I guess I better read that too, since neither of you looks like a white-collar worker."

We ignored that. Sister Ida began.

Local Section American Chemical Society
April 20, 1958

DEAR MOTHER ELSA,

This year the Local Section of ACS has inaugurated a new Honor. Annually we will reward an outstanding chemist of the section and will style that person as the local section's "Chemist of the Year."

"I know that," I interrupted.

"Well, wait. You have no patience at all."

"Go on!" I really was impatient by then. I wanted to check the glassware.

Sister Ida continued:

The award is made on the basis of the individual's contribution to the teaching of chemistry and or research activities, publications and services to the local section. This year . . .

"I know that, too."

Sister Alberta looked at me in disgust.

Sister Ida continued to ignore me.

I stirred uneasily.

Sister Ida resumed:

This year, our "Chemist of the Year" is a Roman Catholic Sister . . .

"It is?" I said, at last interested. "Sister Ida, you're wonderful."

"Silly! You never let me finish anything! Always interrupting! I will reread."

By that time Sister Alberta was looking over Sister Ida's shoulder. "Sister Jeremy, it's you!"

"Never! Can't be! What did I do?"

"Well, Sister Jeremy." Sister Ida cleared her throat. "We will not list everything lest you become worldly, but a few will not hurt: charter member of the section, member of the board since its foundation, held office of secretary, treasurer, vice-president, chairman of the student committee. Those are a few examples."

"This can't be. And if you are fooling . . ."

"Read it yourself." Sister Ida finally lost patience and thrust the letter in front of me.

I laughed. "You know, after all these years I finally got you to be impatient, Sister Ida."

Then all three of us laughed.

Sister Alberta took the letter from me and exclaimed, "Look at the note at the bottom—from Mother Elsa!"

"You never did let me finish! Read it to us please, Sister Alberta."

Sister Miriam and Sister Alberta will accompany Sister Jeremy to the annual banquet of the Local ACS to receive the plaque honoring the Chemist of the Year.

"Well, if I could use slang, I know many things I could say, but I am speechless. To think of all the worthy chemists among the 200 members of the local section and they chose me."

It was a golden era for the chemistry department. Through these wholesome contacts Federal and private laboratories applied to us for science editors, librarians, technologists. Our students were certain of positions before graduation. Added to our satisfaction was the growing number of science students who gave us the very best kind of help—*they joined our ranks.* How happily did Sister Ida, Sister Alberta and I watch as our Anns and Ellens became Sister Sixtus, Sister Aelred, Sister Coleman. . . .

God was indeed blessing us. The students became more and more devoted to St. Albert, whom the Church had recently canonized, proclaimed a doctor and the patron of natural sciences. Sister Alberta was a great "press agent" of his.

But our old limitations of space were still with us. For several semesters we had been using St. Albert Hall not only for freshmen, but also for the seniors in chemistry. The "temporary" patch had worn threadbare!

Quite suddenly events mushroomed! The community undertook the building of a new academy west of Tannerton on St. Michael's property. The high school, which had always occupied the north wing of Scotus Hall on Coxwil Avenue and shared the gymnasium, chapel and campus facilities with the college, was moved in less than two years. With immense pleasure Mother Elsa announced the plan to renovate the vacated wing completely for the use of the college. A hand-me-down to be sure, but Padua had always proved itself able to "make the best of what we have."

The renovation was well planned and executed. All departments of the scholastic building except the library—and the chemistry department—were moved to the shining new quarters. Spacious as the renovated wing had become, there was "not room in the inn" for all of us. An important consideration in the decision to retain chemistry in the scholastic wing was the fact that Scotus Hall is so shaped that the chemical fumes would permeate the whole building. Mother Elsa was apologetic about the situation, and I knew our plight was in the forefront of her mind. But with the added financial burden of the remodeling, I did not dare to hope for relief before five or ten years.

"Sister Alberta, this is really quite nice," I said, glancing up from my stack of notebooks as we sat at our desks in the old chem lab.

"You mean the ultraprivacy we have, now that the other classes are in the Coxwil wing?" she asked, poising her red ballpoint over a page. "I guess we are a pretty good example of 'happiness does not lie in material things.'"

"No, I was thinking about the new infirmary for our sick and retired Sisters, which the council decided to build. If the community can't afford a big enough place for us to work in, at least it is going to make sure we'll have a nice place to retire in!"

"Retire! Sister Jeremy, how can you be thinking of that?" she chided. "You have years and years ahead of you yet!"

"Maybe! If it will take ten years to pay the present debt and ten more for the infirmary debt, I'll bet I'm a weary-boned old inmate of the new infirmary before the chem department moves into adequate quarters."

Sister Alberta was afraid to gainsay me on that, but neither of us suspected how God in His goodness, His saints, Sister Olivia, and, of course, Mother Regina too, were preparing to surprise us. Only two years after the move to the Coxwil wing, Mother Elsa came to our January faculty meeting and dropped a veritable bomb with the words: "Members of the faculty of Padua College, the board deems it an absolute necessity, in spite of pressing financial difficulties, to erect a science unit which will house the departments of chemistry, natural science and health education."

The room gyrated giddily. I dimly heard the plans outlined and the reactions of the faculty. My knees buckled; after the meeting I tried to get up and walk. Sister Alberta was bubbling incoherently in an effort to help me come to. Others of the faculty kindly congratulated us. God is good, I thought. Where the money would come from we did not know. We put our trust in God and knew that He Who had thus blessed our dream would see us over the financial hurdle. It seemed a good thing to enlist the services of that heavenly carpenter and old friend of the community, St. Joseph, for "Operation Dream Come True." Beside his statue in the lecture room we also placed one of the girl martyr, St. Philomena, known to possess uncanny powers over the purse. Students watched this brief ritual quizzically, then someone got it.

"Sister Jeremy! Sister Alberta! Does it really mean—honest?"

"What do you think?" Sister Alberta teased.

In response, a deafening jargon of delight, mingled with aspirations to the two Saints, rocked the room.

That same day a note in my mailbox read:

SISTER JEREMY:

You and Sister Alberta will draw up plans for a two-story science unit adequate for five hundred students in chemistry, natural science and health education. We would like to break ground in April. You have my permission to visit other college science buildings to glean ideas.

Devotedly,
MOTHER ELSA

This was the beginning of the second semester, February 1. On our heels came the architect who had also received his orders. We had to think of the most practical and most economical, but at the same time, most efficient plan.

We measured and drew and measured again. After four weeks we had blueprints for lecture rooms, laboratories, instrument and balance rooms, faculty and student research rooms. Soon the architect and we too had strung out plans for miles of piping for steam, hot and cold water, electric wiring of various voltages, gas connections and a vacuum. . . .

A curious circumstance in preparing for the ground breaking was finding the shovel used in the ground-breaking ceremony of Scotus Hall. Hand-carved on its wooden handle was the still legible inscription: SCOTUS HALL, 1922. MOTHER M. REGINA, O.S.F. Polished to a mirrorlike brilliancy and gaily decked with ribbons and flowers, it served again to make history at Padua on that memorable April Sunday, the feast of Our Lady of Good Counsel. We had asked Mother Elsa to give Sister Ida the honor of turning over the first shovelful. Sister Ida was delighted to the point of tears. This had always been her dream. Never in all the years of her excellent teaching had she enjoyed adequate accommodations from St. Albert's to Padua. St. Joseph was placed in the contractor's trailer to oversee the work. "Operation Dream Come True" was under way!

Epilogue

"*Jubilate Deo!*" Another June, another Jubilee Day! What made this one special was the fact that Sister Ida was celebrating her golden anniversary of religious profession, and I—Sister Jeremy (was it possible?)—was a silver jubilarian! It was a day of community-wide rejoicing. Sister Ida and I could scarcely find words to express our gratitude to God. We were experiencing all the beautiful ceremonies and congratulations we had so often witnessed and expressed for our Sisters through the years.

Sitting on the community porch in the evening after some of the excitement had died down, we two "friends from old" traded memories, from the early days at St. Albert's to our "Dream Come True." We talked mostly of our companion Sisters—dear old Sister Bonaventure, gone now these five years to her reward; Sister Basil with her strictness and sincerity; Sister Martin, the lovable joker; Sister Patrick with her delightful brogue; Sister Marie of that unforgettable baseball game; Sister Cosma, Sister Serene and all the rest. What good times we had had! Odd, how we never tired of recounting them on campus each summer as we met again for retreat. We talked of our students, wondered and worried about them, laughed all over again at the funny things they had done and said. Red, Pete, Eugenia, Fred, Dorothy, Jack, Ann—class after class—appeared again in fancy's eye. How were they all now? we wondered. They would never be erased from our memories—nor our prayers. We looked forward to that day of eternal reunion with the God of all Love. What a grand get-together it would be!

One of our greatest satisfactions was the continued interest and affection of our Padua graduates. Out in all fields of science and teaching, or setting up a beautiful Christian family life, they sent back frequent notes and letters filled with homey and sometimes exciting experiences that brightened many a recreation.

Students in further study related ins and outs of university classes:

> ... in chem 452 I'm attempting to isolate A.T.P. creatine transphosphoratose from rabbit muscle ... The whole operation is really on a major scale. In one place we use over forty liters of $NaHCo_3$ ...

> The physical chem exam comes up Tuesday. I hope you'll be praying for me. You know how I need it ...

From the other side of the desk, our alumnae teachers shared their experiences:

> My engineers had their first hour exam yesterday, and the class median was 91. Believe me, it's not my teaching—I just have a smart group of fellows. But my freshmen have their exams tonight. I'm afraid they're doomed—I am too, because we'll be grading exams till midnight ...

> My chemistry classes are making crystals, and finding it as much fun as I did ...

Our "family" women bubbled through pages of babies' antics:

> Here is my son—the sweetest, dearest little fellow one could ever hope to have. He loves all animals—maybe we should have called him Francis ...

> We've really been blessed, Sister—another fine healthy boy! Katie too is very well—now has her *fifth* girl!

But all the letters are characterized by one feature: deep, sincere, appreciation for the days at Padua:

> I take pride in my Catholic liberal arts education. It is a tremendous influence for good in daily life and I thank God for it....

Such devoted loyalty and sincere affection formed no small part of our "hundredfold" in this life. As we sat in the twilight, speared by the last shafts of sun, I turned to Sister Ida. "It's been a golden day...."

"And the future is bright!" she added with her still youthful smile.

The future . . . Would I someday say "America, I'm off for India?" Chemistry at Padua is still my appointment, but in my heart the flame of hope flickers constantly—someday, India. But no matter where, India or Tannerton, always I would wear His ring, a reminder of the vows I had taken "in order to do penance, to amend my life, to serve God faithfully until death."

. . . until death doth unite us eternally. Love is eternal. Love is a consecration.

You wouldn't believe me if I had told you the truth. You couldn't. Besides, I do not think I could have told it to you, not articulately. Oh, I am so much in love. A gold ring on my left hand serves as a constant reminder of my unending devotion to Christ.